MED/BIO

AVERAGE
EXPECTATIONS

AVERAGE EXPECTATIONS

Lessons in Lowering the Bar

SHEP ROSE

WITH DINA GACHMAN

GALLERY BOOKS

New York London Toronto Sydney New Delhi

G

Gallery Books
An Imprint of Simon & Schuster, Inc.
1230 Avenue of the Americas
New York, NY 10020

First Gallery Books hardcover edition March 2021

Photos in text courtesy of the author.

GALLERY BOOKS and colophon are registered trademarks
of Simon & Schuster, Inc.

For information about special discounts for bulk purchases,
please contact Simon & Schuster Special Sales at 1-866-506-1949
or business@simonandschuster.com.

The Simon & Schuster Speakers Bureau can bring authors
to your live event. For more information or to book an event,
contact the Simon & Schuster Speakers Bureau at 1-866-248-3049
or visit our website at www.simonspeakers.com.

Interior design by Jaime Putorti

Manufactured in the United States of America

10   9   8   7   6   5   4   3   2   1

Library of Congress Cataloging-in-Publication Data

Names: Rose, Shep, author.
Title: Average expectations : lessons in lowering the bar / Shep Rose; with Dina Gachman.
Description: First Gallery Books hardcover edition. | New York : Gallery Books, 2021.
Identifiers: LCCN 2020044100 (print) | LCCN 2020044101 (ebook) | ISBN 9781982159795
    (hardcover) | ISBN 9781982159801 (paperback) | ISBN 9781982159818 (ebook)
Subjects: LCSH: Rose, Shep. | Southern charm (Television program) | Television personalities—
    United States—Biography. | Reality television programs—United States. | Conduct of life. |
    Southern States—Social life and customs.
Classification: LCC PN1992.4.R578 A3 2021 (print) | LCC PN1992.4.R578 (ebook) |
    DDC 791.4502/8092 [B]—dc23
LC record available at https://lccn.loc.gov/2020044100
LC ebook record available at https://lccn.loc.gov/2020044101

ISBN 978-1-9821-5979-5
ISBN 978-1-9821-5981-8 (ebook)

For Josh Adams, Randy Light, and Jane Furtado

"It is a tale told by an idiot, full of sound and fury, signifying nothing."
—Shakespeare

. . . . . .

Hobbes: So, the secret to good self-esteem is to lower your expectations to the point where they're already met?
Calvin: Right. We should take pride in our mediocrity.

CONTENTS

· INTRODUCTION ·

WELCOME TO SHEPLAND

Writing requires discipline. It means you're sitting alone for long periods of time instead of being out there in the world having fun, with a babe on one side and a beer or two on the other. Or a babe on each side holding a beer *for* you. Or two babes on each side . . . you get the picture.

So why the hell am I doing this?

I had it made! As I write this, I'm entering the seventh season of filming *Southern Charm*. I've got a few side investments and companies (or "hustles," if you want to make it all sound culturally relevant and cool). I was happy and lazy sitting on the beach in Charleston, living in "Shepland," which is a magical place devoid of stress and full of beer and good times. The name came from an older guy who owned a pizza place in my hometown (for which I

v), and he made it up in honor of yours truly. In
matters and there are no consequences. Every-
work out, and being blissfully average is the
goal. I've spent my entire life there, lowering the bar, with very few
interruptions. Until now.

So why make the choice to suddenly give myself deadlines and
responsibility and work?

Being on reality TV means that strangers might know my
name, or they might call me an asshole on social media. That's
when you really know you've "made it." But it doesn't exactly
mean I'm sitting atop the television industry as far as prestige
goes. It's not like people confuse Shep Rose with Daniel Day-
Lewis. On second thought, maybe I *am* the Daniel Day-Lewis of
reality TV? Someone so deep into the character that the character
is . . . ME?

Plus, I have had a pretty darn good education for someone who
strives for blissful mediocrity. I refuse to rest on my laurels, though,
as mildly impressive as they are. In any case, dammit, it's high time
I put pen to paper before my life stories are swept into the dustbin
of time. That would be a tragedy, as you'll see when you (hopefully)
continue reading this book.

Never in a million years did I envision that I would be on
a show like *Southern Charm*. I never imagined I would work in
entertainment at all. You see, in the South, where I was born and
bred and still live, you'd literally get laughed off the screened-in
porch if you said you were going to try to make it in Hollywood.
Even hinting at a minuscule interest in theater was met with a

skeptical side-eye. It was generally accepted and expected that you grow up to be a banker, a lawyer, a doctor, or a real estate magnate. My family is full of esteemed people who were way above average: a great-aunt who was the first female athlete on the cover of *Time* magazine, grandfathers and uncles who were decorated soldiers or revered businesspeople, lawyers, and politicians who mingled with world leaders. And then there's me, Shep: reality TV personality and all-around average guy. Although being average isn't so bad, as I'll prove in these pages.

Is there an alternate universe where I'm an investment banker? I mean, it wouldn't have been *that* unlikely, considering how I grew up. If I had become a banker or lawyer, I would have basically been playing a role in a movie. At least on *Southern Charm* I can just be Shep. In my twenties, I went down that road for a minute, but I had an epiphany on a trip to Hong Kong (more on that later) and realized that I would never be that guy in the suit saddled with responsibility, tied down, and having zero fun. Around that time, one of my dad's friends told me that nothing matters before you're thirty, so I've just stretched that to forty. Maybe I'll push it to fifty. Right now, I'm just a guy out there in the world trying to amuse himself. It's not a bad role to play, but it pisses some people off . . . typically the "misery loves company" sort.

I went to school with varying degrees of success. I was a straight B student. I studied the night before and pretty much skated by, and eventually my parents learned that I had what you could call a behavioral problem. You see, I may have been patient zero for ADD and ADHD; I forgot which one I had/have (which is classic

ADD/ADHD). When I was in fourth grade, my family was living in Alexandria, Virginia, because my dad was working for the Reagan administration (again, above average!), and my mom and my teachers agreed that I might need to be examined by some behavioral specialists. My mom took me to a doctor, and they put me in a room with a table and a chair and told me to take a test. Little did I know there was a two-way mirror behind which I'm assuming sat Manhattan Project–caliber scientists, watching and studying little Shep, mouths agape at what they were witnessing.

After the allotted hour, my mom was asked to talk to the lead scientist (aka a child psychologist). Just for some context, this was around 1988, so Ritalin was in its infancy and was being wildly overprescribed. So, the good doctor pulls my mom aside and this is what ensues:

> *Doctor: We have good news and bad news.*
> *Mom: Tell me the good news first.*
> *Doctor: He did very well on the test.*
> *Mom: The bad news?*
> *Doctor: He laid on his back on the floor underneath the table with the test stuck to the underside of the metal table. We have never seen anyone take a test that way before . . .*

This might actually be my first taste of stardom: I was going to be featured in medical journals around the world!

After the test, I was prescribed what the legendary drug-loving drummer Levon Helm would call "an adult portion" of Ritalin to take before school. Don't get me wrong, the drug did help me focus, but I hated who it turned me into. My whole personality changed. At first the teachers were probably relieved to have a mild-mannered child in their class instead of a hellion, but then I think they started to have second thoughts. I distinctly remember my sixth-grade math class being right before lunch. I refused to leave the classroom unless I understood everything that the teacher had just spent the last hour teaching, plus I would argue and question everything she said. I'm sure the poor woman just wanted to have a cigarette and a sandwich, but I wouldn't leave. At least without Ritalin I would have given the teacher a break.

When I finally did leave for lunch, I would walk into the cafeteria and my friends would call me over to sit with them. And totally out of character for a social butterfly/troublemaker like myself, I wouldn't, or rather couldn't. I would sit by myself and NOT eat my lunch. Actually, I would just eat the Shark Bites fruit snacks in my lunch box (saving the great whites for last, of course) because in addition to robbing me of my charisma, the Ritalin also robbed me of hunger. I was irritated by my friends, highly antisocial, and unable to inhabit Shepland. I hated the drug and stopped taking it in high school, where I resumed my normal activities of raising hell and having fun.

Signs of my innate rebelliousness, nonconformity, and burgeoning averageness were everywhere from the very start. My poor mom probably wasn't surprised by any doctor's observations or diagnoses. When I was just two years old, there were a series of incidents that were harbingers of things to come. For one thing, my parents had to lock me inside the house or I'd escape. I had just learned to walk and apparently had places to go and people to see. And in one case, garden utensils to steal.

One day, a friend of my mom's came over and my mom forgot to lock the door, and so I plotted my escape and toddled out of the house undetected. My mom and her friend frantically ran around outside screaming my name until they spotted me dragging a rake and a hoe down the street. I guess I had gone to a neighbor's garage and absconded with some tools to assist with my developing green thumb. Or maybe I just wanted to dig some holes and create havoc. My mom was too embarrassed to knock on doors and return the tools, so she just left them leaning against the neighbors' mailboxes and took me home. If you were a Rose neighbor circa 1982 through 1995, please submit a detailed financial breakdown of what I owe you and Simon & Schuster will reimburse you directly.

Another time, my grandmother was visiting, and she left the back door open (you see where this is going). The back door opened up to a fairway of a golf course, which we all know is extremely dangerous terrain (alligators, wayward heat-seeking golf balls, etc.). Anyway, there were some roofers at our house fixing shingles that day. My mom and grandmother couldn't find me anywhere until some golfers came screaming up our lawn, saying they spied a tiny person on top of the house. I was sitting cross-legged on the roof laughing my little ass off, staring certain death in the face. The roofers must have been on lunch break. How I got up there, I have no idea. I've always been wily, and to be honest I'm impressed with my two-year-old self for his acrobatic antics.

The final story, or maybe the last one my mom is willing to tell before she bursts into retroactive tears from all the anxiety I caused, is when I was almost three years old and she walked into the kitchen and I had somehow climbed onto the top of the refrigerator. I literally had my hand in the cookie jar. As my mom tells it, we locked eyes, then I screamed and jumped off the fridge from six feet up, landing on my feet and running to the living room to hide underneath the couch. Because I hadn't hurt myself leaping off the fridge, my mom was too shocked to punish me. In many ways, I have never changed. I made a conscious decision back then to remain that kid leaping off the fridge and courting middling danger at every turn, and so far, I've been pretty successful.

My mom always thought I was like the kid from *Where the Wild Things Are*, but I always felt more like Calvin from the comic strip *Calvin and Hobbes*. He was my earliest hero. He was analytical and cynical. He had untapped potential (meaning he hovered around mediocre on a daily basis, like me), a hatred for authority, and a mischievous streak. Bill Watterson, who created the comic, said of Calvin: "I wouldn't want Calvin in my house, but on paper, he helps me sort through my life and understand it." I think he was giving Calvin a compliment.

My mom looked at me early on and said, "If you can't beat him, join him." She bought me every *Calvin and Hobbes* comic, probably because she related to Calvin's mom. That comic actually taught me more than I learned in school in some ways. My mom helped foster my rebellious spirit and taught me ways to channel it into more thought-provoking contrarianism rather than lawless and dangerous behavior. I have always been acutely aware of the difference between right and wrong, and I always felt like my mom and dad and grandparents were watching, and I dare not embarrass them . . . at least not too much.

Since I was a toddler, I guess, I've had a deep respect for renegades, contrarians, and disruptors. People who didn't care about social restrictions or traditions. Adventurers who carved their own way. I like people who "get the joke"—the joke being life. These are people like Hunter S. Thompson, Keith Richards, Falstaff, Ernest Hemingway, the surfer Bunker Spreckels. Here's the thing: There are always people who bitch and moan about rules being broken and precedents being set, but the people who actually make history are the ones who give the world the middle finger. I've tried to live my life that way, by giving the finger instead of doing what's expected, and sometimes it works—and sometimes people get pissed. And I'm okay with that. I'm also not sure I'm making history, but I do have some great stories.

I guess I'm writing this book to inspire you to get in on the joke and give someone the middle finger instead of doing what you're supposed to—within reason, of course. I *was* raised by Southern gentlemen and ladies, so I try to have manners, but my manners might be laced with a little whiskey-induced devilry from time to time. I'll tell you stories about women and wine and mushrooms. I'll talk about my dog, Lil Craig. I'll regale you with insane travel tales and ridiculous work experiences that helped me figure out who I am *not*, and that ultimately led me to *Southern Charm*. Yes, I'll talk about the show, but I mainly want to talk about living life off the leash, totally free to do whatever I want, even at forty. A life where setting average expectations for yourself is actually pretty glorious. Am I slowing down and contemplating a more traditional type of life? Maybe. Do I imagine settling down one day? We'll see . . .

For now, I'm just here to show you a good time.

I can promise that these stories will be wildly entertaining, because they're coming from a guy who got the "Enthusiasm Award" in fourth grade. This was the same year I was cast (without even having to audition, I might add) as Tigger the tiger in our school production of *Winnie-the-Pooh*. My only line was: "Bouncing is what Tigger does best!" Even though I was typecast, it prepared me for my later one-liner as an ambulance driver in the Bruce Willis movie *Reprisal*. My line was: "When's the last time she ate!" The movie went straight to DVD.

Besides my Enthusiasm Award, my Tigger role, and my intense need for freedom and escape as a toddler, the childhood incident that most predicted the trajectory of my adult life happened in the seventh grade, when Mrs. Sabo wrote a note to my parents on my report card that said: *Shep thinks he can get through seventh grade on charm alone . . . He doesn't have that much.*

And on that note, ladies and gentlemen, welcome to Shepland.

AVERAGE
EXPECTATIONS

· CHAPTER 1 ·

NOT-SO-HUMBLE BEGINNINGS

When I was kicking around potential titles for this book, I proposed and fought for a few. I was irrationally and a little jokingly telling the powers that be that when the book was published, I should be touted as the next Charles Dickens! The voice of a generation! A literary and creative force of nature!

Dejected by their lack of enthusiasm, I said fine, we can call it *Average Expectations*—an obvious tip of the cap to the great Charles Dickens, but also an admission of defeat. But there is another layer to the title. Some would say a double entendre of sorts. Because the following is true: I come from a line that includes some amazingly accomplished and interesting people. I've been blessed to have family members who were war heroes, world travelers, captains

1

of industry, famous socialites, Jazz Age female golfers, friends of F. Scott Fitzgerald's, a federal judge, along with a slew of eccentric, strange, and hilarious relatives in the bunch.

And then there's me: reality television boozehound and international lothario.

How proud everyone must be! If there's truly such a thing as rolling over in one's grave, I'm sure my ancestors are tied in knots by now. Whatever "great expectations" existed for me have been imploded over the years by my constant lowering of the bar. I never thought much about family name or placed much importance on it, but Lord knows in the South and New England and in places like Palm Beach it's like actual currency for some people. (I *have* been interested to meet a Rockefeller or Vanderbilt or Du Pont, mostly because it's American history, which is fascinating to me.) Family names mean a great deal to some, but it's so shallow and silly. It does bother me when online trolls come at me by saying I inherited everything I have, or making it seem like I should feel guilty because of my family and what they worked for. So, people who walk around trumpeting who they are and where they come from are ridiculous, but I also understand the irony of me dedicating a chapter to my amazing relatives. I'm just trying to give you some context and paint an interesting picture, dammit.

For fun and a hint of pride and braggadocio, I now present to you a few branches of my family tree that prove that even though I may not be worthy of the Presidential Medal of Freedom, at least some of my relatives could be. My section at

Medieval Times did win the whole jousting tournament once in Myrtle Beach, but that's probably not as impressive as *actual* war medals.

MOM'S SIDE

"Grains to Trains: The Story of Christopher Cummings" appeared in the above issue of *Fortune.*

Columbus Cummings:

My great-great-great-grandfather was from New England, and he was one of seven children. He was told by his parents to go west when he was twenty years old, so he headed to Illinois. He was in the dry goods business but then decided to go to Southern Illinois, where he met his future wife, Sarah Mark. He opened a dry goods store of his own and did well, and in his spare time he got into farming with his in-laws. He was instrumental in developing the city of Pekin, Illinois. Then, in his forties, he moved to Chicago and put a syndicate together to build the nickel-plated railroad that ran from Toledo to Cleveland to Chicago, and down to St. Louis. He was president of the company, and eventually sold the company to Cornelius Vanderbilt, of THE Vanderbilts. Just thinking of his work ethic makes me want to take a long nap.

Aunt Edith Cummings:
Sister to my great-grandfather (I'll get to PaPa in a second). Edith was so exceptional I decided to google her so I wouldn't miss anything. Here's her Wikipedia bio: "Edith Cummings Munson, popularly known as The Fairway Flapper, was an American socialite and one of the premier amateur golfers during the Jazz Age. She was one of the Big Four debutantes in Chicago during World War I. She attained fame in the United States following her 1923 victory in the U.S. Women's Amateur. On August 25, 1924, she became the first golfer and first female athlete to appear on the cover of *Time* magazine." She also was friendly with F. Scott Fitzgerald, and it's widely agreed that the character Jordan Baker from *The Great Gatsby* was based on Edith. So, you can see, definitely not average.

Dexter Cummings (PaPa):
From Chicago, attended Yale, where he was a two-time NCAA Champion golfer. His father, D. Mark Cummings, died when PaPa was in his early twenties, so he quickly had to manage the family business and grow it, which he did with great success. He was an entrepreneur,

financier, philanthropist, and great sportsman. Once his knees failed him, he focused on saltwater fishing. He had a yacht in Cuba called *Necoya* that was seized by Castro's new regime and appropriated by the Cuban navy. PaPa was once invited to Augusta National when it was first built, and his playing partner was the great Bobby Jones. Jones apparently was miffed that he was giving up so many strokes to an opponent. PaPa supposedly said of that experience, "It didn't matter because I had lots of birdies that day and we won the match!"

He married Emily Hoyt, and they had three daughters, the oldest of which is my grandmother. They lived in Lake Forest, and my grandmother eventually attended Vassar, where she met my grandfather Truman Hobbs.

Judge Truman Hobbs:
My grandfather Gramps was one of my favorite people in the world, and I'm not alone in that. You'd be hard-pressed to find a smarter, kinder, and funnier person who has ever lived! He grew up in Selma, Alabama, and his father was a U.S. senator. Gramps went to UNC Chapel Hill, where he was president of the student body and on the swim team (he was six five, so that helped). He then joined the navy at the onset of World War II. He started as a salvage diver and did his practice diving in the East River in New York City (it was a little cleaner back then).

He then rose to be the commander of a salvage ship. He was on both fronts during the war, was awarded the Navy and Marine Corps Medal and the Bronze Star, and he had so many crazy and funny stories from that time and life that my dad wrote a book chronicling his life. After the war, he attended Yale Law School, and that's when he met my grandmother (NaNa). He applied to be a clerk for the U.S. Supreme Court and got the job, under Justice Hugo Black. After a successful law career, he was nominated by President Jimmy Carter for a federal judgeship back in his native Alabama, where he served on the bench for thirty years. He and NaNa had two girls and two boys, one of which is my mom (hi, Mom!).

Two stories about Gramps I want to share, because he was the best: When he was on a train coming back to Selma after four years of fighting during WWII, he knew his family was eagerly waiting, and this was especially true of his mother. So, he was on the train and saw a young woman with a new baby in her arms. He had an idea—he politely introduced himself to the woman and asked if she could kindly do him a favor. She asked what that might be. He requested that she walk off the train in Selma arm in arm with him while he carried her baby, to mess with his family (especially his mom) and make them think he had gotten married and had a kid overseas without telling them. She happily complied (he was a charmer), and his poor mother fainted right there at the depot. The apple doesn't fall too far from the tree, and at least I take after him in some very important ways.

And this story makes me emotional every time I think of it:

When I was fourteen years old, Gramps was doing a crossword puzzle (he did the *New York Times* puzzle every day—definitely above average) and he asked me if I knew a four-letter word for *paradise* (looking back, it was *Eden*). I immediately replied, "*HOME.*" I saw him tear up, and then so did I. He figured that was a pretty beautiful answer because it meant he had raised a daughter who raised a son who equated home with paradise. After all the laughs and golf rounds, this story is what I remember the most.

DAD'S SIDE

Southern Charm has covered how my family on my dad's side has deep roots in Boykin, South Carolina (the town is named after us, the Boykins). King George granted the land to a distant (like, really distant) relative in the late 1700s. They called it Boykin and the clan grew from there. There are so many different cousins, uncles, and aunts, it could make your head spin. One cool fun fact is that my ancestors were big duck-hunters, but the Labradors they used to fetch the ducks were capsizing the boats they were sitting in, so they created a breed called Boykin spaniels, and that breed became the state dog of South Carolina.

Camden, South Carolina, is right next door and became a horse racing and horse farm mecca earlier in the twentieth century, which brought some big money and prestige to the area, which was mostly all about farming before that point. The horse racing scene brought partiers from New York and beyond to this small farming town, and apparently there were some radical parties in Camden/ Boykin back in the day, which is how my grandparents and then my parents actually met.

Papa (yes, another Papa):

My dad's dad was named Bill Rose. His family owned and ran a huge cypress mill in Perry, Florida. His father died at the young age of fifty-four, so Papa moved to Jacksonville, Florida, with his sister, attended prep schools like Bolles School and then Phillips Exeter, then went on to Cornell University. After his second year he joined WWII in the services of the U.S. Army under none other than General George Patton. Papa became a sergeant in a tank division and fought and helped win in the Battle of the Bulge. It was while in Europe that he made up his mind that he wanted to come back and become an international businessman. He returned to Cornell, got his degree in economics, and joined Armco Steel out of Middletown, Ohio. His willingness to travel sent him first to Paris for a spell and then to Genoa, Italy. My dad grew up in Italy during his formative years, and that's where he got his nickname that stuck for the rest of his life, Rip Rose, named after Rip Van Winkle, who slept for twenty years straight. His Italian nannies had never seen anyone sleep so much. Again, the apple doesn't fall far from the tree! My dad's family eventually came back to Boykin and built a house on my grandmother's family land, and that's where Papa and Dad taught me to hunt, fish, and get cars stuck in the mud (that last one was self-taught, actually). I still go there today and love running into Boykins all over the state.

Great-Uncle Richard "Dixie" Boykin: A very interesting, colorful character. My dad described him this way: "He wasn't in the movies or anything, but he was definitely an entertainer. Big personality. When all the wealthy industrialists from New York came down to the horse farms and parties in Camden in the winter, Dixie was the guy they all sent a telegram to basically saying please prepare for our arrival and set up some big extravagant parties. He was a local bon vivant essentially, and a party facilitator." For some reason I'm picturing the jolly guy in *Moulin Rouge* who runs the cabaret. Anyway, in the 1930s, he went out to Hollywood and tried to break into the motion picture business with varying degrees of success, and he became friends with classic screen star Tallulah Bankhead.

Dixie had a friend called Max Ferguson, from a wealthy Philadelphia family. At the time, gasoline was rationed and scarce. It was hard to farm without gasoline-powered machinery, so it was Dixie's idea to look into getting an elephant to plow the fields instead of a horse or mule. He heard of a circus that was going out of business in Atlanta, so he and Max went down there and purchased Alice the elephant. They arranged to put Alice on a train to Camden. When Alice arrived, much of the town was on horseback and it was a bustling Saturday. When the elephant was unloaded, the horses and mules (and most of the people) had never seen one, and the animals freaked out and caused a stampede through town.

Everyone was upset. So, a law was passed that still stands today in Camden: *No elephants are allowed to be delivered to the train station on Saturdays!*

This experience rightly taught him that elephants, horses, and mules generally don't get along. They also had trouble getting people to guide and work Alice in the field, so Alice became a pet. The eight-thousand-pound elephant in the corner of the room, to the great delight of many around Camden. A couple of years later they sold Alice back to the same circus, which had re-formed.

Finally, my family tree would not be complete without Rip and Fran, my parents, who have put up with me for over forty years . . .

Rip and Fran Rose:
Married over forty-eight years. I hold my dad in as high esteem as Gramps. I'm also not alone on that. We are nothing alike, though. My dad told me he got so drunk once in college that he didn't drink again for three months—what a rookie! He's thoughtful, cautious, a great listener, and very calm and deliberate. He's also one of the fairest and most decent people you'll ever meet. And he loves silly jokes and movies like *Naked Gun*. He worked in the Reagan administration in the tax division and then moved to Hilton Head and spent most of his professional life with the same law firm as a tax and corporate attorney. I give him a hard time (all dads should be given a hard time), we have lots of lively banter, we argue about politics, and we go on amazing fishing trips around the world. Love you, Dad.

My mom is more like me. She can talk and theorize all day and night and loves a good party. (Dad actually likes a good party, too, his college sabbatical notwithstanding.) She is also basically solely responsible for raising me and my two siblings. She did everything—school, practices, making us study and write thank-you notes, cooking dinner, challenging us mentally, organizing all holidays and family trips, taking us to the emergency room (in my case a lot), and much, much more. She is truly the person who makes me think that home is paradise. Love you, Mom.

Shep-Approved
SOUTHERN TRADITIONS

While I am not an authority on being a Southern gentleman, I was reared in the South, so I know a thing or two. Many of the traditions should go the way of Betamax tapes and the guillotine, but some are okay. Here are a few that I think every man should abide by:

1. Never ask a woman her age at a party, and DEFINITELY do not ask a woman if she's pregnant! (I made this mistake once before, and I'm still mortified.)

2. Hold the door open. It's a simple gesture, but it's a small display of humanity and courtesy, and these days we can use as much of that as we can get.

3. Let people over in traffic. Like anyplace, the South has their fair share of asshole drivers, but far less so than in the Northeast and Florida and Los Angeles (sue me). By the way, Florida and Texas are not the South, they're their own entities. Come at me if you must.

4. Saying "darling" and "honey" and "sweetie" to everyone you meet. I wondered about this tradition after the Me Too movement.

I even tweeted about it after a nice older lady at an airport Burger King gave me a burger and said, "Have a good day, honey!" I replied, "You too, darling!" Afterward I polled the internet and almost everyone agreed that if initiated with a playfulness by (typically) the woman, it is uniquely Southern and totally acceptable to say things like "darling." And thank goodness, because it's a tradition I love.

5. Standing when a lady comes to a table, helping her into her coat, and pulling out a chair. I'm not always the best at this because I get excited/distracted and I forget sometimes. But it's a nice, quaint thing, and my mom likes it, and women should be treated with more reverence than men. They run the world, after all. Or at least, they should.

6. Saying "yes, ma'am"/"no, sir" to elders. I still do this in most situations. Respect is never a bad thing to offer, unless the elder is a jerk, in which case, you can nix this rule.

7. Cotillion dance classes. I was thrown out of mine at age twelve for borrowing a girl's white gloves and slapping my friends across the face with them, but I did learn the foxtrot, so there's that.

· CHAPTER 2 ·

IN ON THE JOKE

Despite my family tree, expectations in life were fairly low for me, which is a hell of a good position to be in. I mean, the potential was always there. I showed glimmers of excellence, but those glimmers were always quickly washed away by waves of tomfoolery.

I followed a traditional path of graduating high school and going to college and then business school, but I never sought out a traditional life. I've been too busy seeking out a good time, which is a lifestyle choice that has a way of leading you to detours and potholes and epic hangovers instead of promotions and corporate expense accounts. Instead of sitting at a desk in a suit, I'm wearing jeans and a T-shirt on TV—and it's considered work. Well, it is by some.

I never imagined that I'd be where I am, but was it my destiny? How did the patient zero of Ritalin, favorite-class-is-recess kid grow up to be on a reality show for six seasons (and counting)?

I'll try to explain. Remember the heartbreaking scene in *Forrest Gump* when his mother is dying and they have a rudimentary conversation about free will and one's path in life? Forrest asks, "What's my destiny, Mama?" And she replies, "You're gonna have to figure that out for yourself." Forrest's destiny leads him to become a star Ping-Pong player, a decorated soldier, a long-distance runner, a shrimping boat captain, and husband of Jenny and dad to little Forrest. My destiny, on the other hand, led me to *Southern Charm*. I am pretty decent at Ping-Pong, but that's where the Gump similarities begin and end. That, and we're both Southern. But that's pretty much it.

I'm not comparing myself to a hero like Forrest Gump, but who on earth could have predicted I'd land where I am now, just like who on earth could have predicted that Forrest would become a valiant soldier carrying Bubba away from enemy fire and getting shot in the buttocks? But once upon a time, about eight years ago, when the show called *Southern Charm* was conceived, my destiny came calling.

Here's how it happened.

Between your first and second years of business school, you're expected to get a summer internship. For a while, I had worked for golfer/entrepreneur Greg Norman's real estate development company in West Palm Beach (more on my laundry list of jobs later). I had given an Australian businessman named David Spencer a tour of some of our real estate projects and we hit it off, bullshitting and laughing (two of my specialties) throughout the tour. Later on, when I was thinking about my summer internship, I reached out to David to see if he knew of anything. At the time, he was running a company in Dubai, so he arranged for me to spend a summer working there (and partying, because it's all about balance). Life lesson here: If you sense someone is a like-minded soul, don't miss the opportunity to break the ice and stay in contact. You never know how far THEY might go in life!

I loved my time in Dubai (more on that later), and when it was over, I was offered to return on a permanent basis for a nice salary. My destiny was to become an international businessman. It was the dream. At least, it was my dad's dream for me. You see, he grew up in Italy and France because his dad was in the international steel business. So really all my travels have been enthusiastically supported by my dad. I love him for many reasons, but I am most thankful for his "go see the world" spirit and support. It has meant everything to me, because learning about other people and cultures infinitely opens one's mind. Anyway, I returned to the U.S. with my chest out, bragging to everyone that I had a job lined up in Dubai. My dad was excited for me. My mom could finally stop worrying, as much as a mother can not worry as their wild-ass son heads to the land of Sharia law for an unspecified amount of time. Life was good. I had just a few more months of school, and then I was off to the Middle East. The cradle of civilization. Mesopotamia. The Tigris and Euphrates. I think these are all in the same vicinity? Who knows? I was going to Dubai.

But then, kind of like Forrest Gump, destiny hit me in the ass. October 2008 came along, a financial crisis happened, the economy crashed, and the party was over, all around the world. Dubai was hit hard because it was predicated on foreign investment and real estate speculation, and overnight the faucet was simply turned off. The company that hired me certainly wasn't worried about a second-year American business school student calling in to check if his offer was still on the table. Everyone there was holding on for dear life. I remember hearing stories about people just leaving their Range Rovers at the Dubai airport and heading back to wherever they came from, never to return. A few of the guys I knew were actually threatened to be arrested if they ever returned since the locals were blaming them for the downfall of civilization.

I heard through the grapevine that the royal family in Dubai was starting to blame the Western businessmen for risking their sovereign fund on development, which was bullshit. They were arm in arm with the West in wanting to create a paradise in the desert. But this isn't about the Dubai royal family or a global economic crisis—small potatoes. This is about me.

I was out of a job, and my future and the future of my classmates was suddenly in limbo. So, like many people at that time, I moved home and tried to figure out my next move. I was stuck at my parents' house with about ten college degrees, give or take. I was over-educated and under-motivated. Well, it wasn't that *I* was under-motivated; it was that companies weren't motivated to hire anyone. This is where my thankfulness and gratitude kick in for being born into a family with means, because I didn't have crushing student loans like so many people. There is a lot of wealth in Hilton Head, where I grew up, but like anywhere, you see disparities. I know I'm fortunate, but I'm also thankful. I don't feel guilty about who and where I come from, though. The only things I feel guilty about are the stupid things I have done, most of which I am divulging in great detail in the pages of this book. So, yes, I was anxious about what I was going to do with my life, but I also didn't have a bank or university with its hand out, wanting a payment—with interest.

I was living in Hilton Head Island, where I grew up. It's a place I can drive around blindfolded (not that I've tried) and that I love dearly—but it's not exactly where you want to be if you're trying to start a career. I mean, yes, there's tourism during the summers (the population goes from 40,000 to 200,000 from winter to summer), but it's like Groundhog Day: same people, same places, every single day. I don't really mind that lifestyle, and I almost prefer it at times. You see, I love walking into a place and knowing a handful of people right off the bat. That's why I never understood the allure of a place like New York City, where you're surrounded by strangers at all times. That's not a lifestyle I seek. I know they say familiarity breeds contempt, but I think whoever said that must have had really annoying friends.

That's why I think Charleston is the perfect place to live: It's not too big and not too small. You can go places and see familiar faces, and maybe also meet someone new every now and then.

But back to Hilton Head Island. As soon as I moved there, my best friend, Andrew, moved from L.A., and so did a handful of old buddies. We had an amazing crew, and nobody was married, so we wreaked havoc on that small island. One friend had a house near the beach, and we would have epic beach days, pounding beers in the sun and grilling out and just trying to one-up each other. I'll always cherish those times. I even briefly dated a cop.

Here's the story. I lost my cell phone one night when we were out, so the next day I asked a friend to call my phone, and a female cop answered. I went to go meet her and wouldn't you know it (or not): She was hot! A hot cop. I was still a little drunk, so I started flirting with her. She said her partner had my phone, so I said, "Well, you should call it." She did, and I was like, "Now I have your number!" Pretty slick. Flirting with the law.

After a month of back-and-forth PG-13 texts (she was a decorated officer, after all), I took her out. Things went well and we hooked up, but after our second date she broke up with me. She said I was too immature and that I asked about the contents of the evidence room too much. It's a damn shame. I'd truly be invincible if I were still sleeping with the LAW!

I did manage to write a business plan during that time that involved raising money to buy distressed homes and waiting until the market returned to sell them. I bought an oceanfront condo at a bankruptcy auction and fixed it up, but the business plan went nowhere. First off, everyone was struggling, and also: Who in their right mind would give ME a bunch of money to invest? Plus, I've always hated sales and asking people for anything, so it just wasn't going to happen. At this point, I was holding on to the hope that my dad's friend's advice that "life doesn't matter before you're thirty" was true.

During this time, I was also going to visit friends around the country to see what they were up to and to see what the hell might be out there job-wise. I remember wanting to make something happen in San Francisco, but nothing materialized. One weekend when I was in Atlanta, I went to a "fast casual" Asian restaurant (think Chipotle but with rice and noodle bowls). I love Asian food in general, and I loved this restaurant, so much so that I got inspired to ask for the owner's name at the counter. Before I knew it, I was trying to become a franchisee of a Tin Drum restaurant. At the same time, I was working on another franchise deal that had me traveling from Hilton Head to Charleston to look for retail space—and of course have a little fun. That's when everything changed.

The date my destiny shifted (again) was New Year's Eve 2012. I was at a rooftop party in Charleston during one of these trips when I spotted Thomas Ravenel. He was a Charleston businessman and politician before he was cast on *Southern Charm*, allowing him to add "reality TV star" to his illustrious résumé. Thomas lived across the street from my uncle, and we were acquaintances. We later actually discovered that we were distant cousins, which isn't all that unusual in South Carolina. Perhaps nowadays a 23andMe DNA test should be required before any Southern wedding, because you never know.

At the rooftop party, I asked Thomas what he was up to, and he said that a guy named Whitney from Los Angeles was in town filming a docuseries about his life in Charleston. Almost on cue, Whitney Sudler-Smith walked across the roof and asked if I knew where any chicks were. I said sure, and then I gave him my go-to business card at that time, which consisted of a picture of a guy punching another guy in the balls with the words "Go Fuck Yourself."

My business card.

It seems he liked my card, because we've been fast friends ever since! That night, Whitney explained that his mom had just moved to Charleston from New York, and while he was visiting her, he observed via some dinner parties that Charleston had a lot of genuine, offbeat, and interesting characters. He said he was in the TV business and he thought the city might be ripe for a TV show celebrating and investigating these colorful Southern characters.

I guess I fit that bill, because after meeting me on the rooftop he said that he and his business partner would like to buy me lunch and talk. We ended up having a hilarious and boozy lunch, and he offered to put me on the show, which is funny, since I was very against reality TV at the time. He needed to put together a "sizzle reel" first (basically a trailer that convinces Hollywood execs to buy an idea), so I told him we could go to my family's farm with a bunch of friends and have some fun, build a fire, shoot some skeet, and drink some whiskey—a pretty standard evening on the farm. We ended up having a blast and getting a taxi to a strip club outside of Columbia, South Carolina, which is always a good idea. After that, I thought I'd never hear from those guys again. Chalk the experience up to my "I'll try anything once" philosophy. Not that I had never been to a strip club before, but I had never taken someone who had offered me a job to a strip club, though it seemed logical at that moment. In case you're wondering, there is footage of that fateful night out there somewhere, but what the hell. If it leaks, it leaks. It's not like I have aspirations to become a politician or a priest.

I actually hated the footage I saw from that night at the farm. I was trying really hard to be provocative and devil-may-care, but I ended up sounding like a dilettante. Some may argue that I *am* a dilettante, but I have since learned to play my cards closer to the chest (mostly). Looking back, I actually learned a valuable lesson from that experience: Don't try too hard in front of the camera, because the camera never lies, and even a casual observer can see through the charade.

After that crazy night, I went back to work on the franchise deal I'd been focused on, and I didn't think about the show at all (well, maybe a little). I figured it was just some Hollywood guy doing what they do best—bullshitting you into believing they're working on something big and taking you with them. Well, six months later I got a call from a manager in L.A. who said he was friends with Whitney and that Bravo loved the show, and that he would be sending me a contract to sign. They said they loved how much of an unabashed nitwit I was on camera. It's painful to think about how cocky I acted at the time, but I had oversold that mystical place of mine called Shepland, which I guess caught the interest of the denizens of La-La Land. I suppose they'd never seen such brazen idiocy. Again, this is why I learned to hold things closer to the vest. Maybe the lesson is: Act like a dumbass, and then when you get their attention, you try to rein it in. (Disclaimer: This advice doesn't apply to bankers, doctors, lawyers, nurses, businesspeople, accountants, or teachers.)

More unsolicited yet valuable advice: When someone in Hollywood says they're sending you a contract, sit back and open a few twelve-packs and a handle of bourbon, because the process takes forever. What followed after that call was six months of back-and-forth between forces more knowledgeable than myself. Frankly, I wasn't all that bullish on the idea in the first place. That may be somewhat hard to reconcile given the fact that I've been on *Southern Charm* for so long, but I was always the snob who scoffed at reality TV. I even scoffed at brainless movies like *The Fast and the Furious* and *Transformers*. Of course I had absolutely no basis for my condescension, but I liked the Coen brothers and Wes Anderson and shows written by Aaron Sorkin. Dark shit that was about as far from popcorn entertainment as you could get. To become what I despised, and for no good reason, gave me pause.

But not that much pause.

I mean, there I was, a thirty-three-year-old business school graduate in the middle of becoming a franchisee of a Tin Drum restaurant out of Atlanta—a deal that had just taken a turn for the worse. And here's where Gump's mom's voice comes in: I was humming along with my deal with the Atlanta folks, and the rug was pulled out from underneath me at the one-yard line, so is fate a thing? Certainly seems like it sometimes. When that deal fell through, I was pretty much open to anything. There was also a part of me that knew I could make people laugh and bring some joie de vivre to the table. I had secretly harbored a desire to do stand-up comedy in college, but to think it and then actually get up there and crack jokes are two separate things, especially when nobody you know is going that route. Remember, I was brought up in a world of traditional Southern expectations, and the University of Georgia, where I went to college, was a place where people (at least the people I hung out with) very much followed those expectations, and stand-up comedy definitely did not fit into this. I mean, sure, Athens has a cool and hip artistic vibe, and my friends and I were insane and we partied harder than anyone, but then we went to economics and finance class the next day (somehow, sometimes).

I know it sounds like I'm making up excuses for why I didn't have the balls to get on a comedy stage, and I kind of am. But compare my world back then to someone like Jonah Hill, who grew up in Los Angeles and had Adam Levine from Maroon 5 as a best friend. In that scene, anything seemed possible to me. Rob Reiner's close friend was the actor/director/comedian Albert Brooks, and Rob's dad was Carl Reiner, one of the greatest comedians of all time. Supposedly Carl thought little Albert was great when he had birthday parties for Rob, and that's how things got started for him. In Hilton Head Island, though, my best friend as a kid was Andrew Carmines, and his parents owned the popular Hilton Head restaurant Hudson's Seafood, and now Andrew runs it (it's amazing, by the way). The point is, famous people in California lived in a different world, and I lived in the South, where connections could get you a corner office or a seafood restaurant, but a comedy career? Hell no.

Since this world was so foreign to me and because I was still a highbrow snob who thought reality shows had as much integrity and creative merit as a Long John Silver's, I asked all my friends and family what I should do. I got a lot of varying responses, many of them negative and some positive. The people who initially told me not to do it have since come back and admitted how wrong they were, which is always validating. But there is one answer that sticks with me to this day and makes me feel like maybe in some ways that I, Shep Rose, am actually a little bit like a real-life Forrest Gump. When I asked my mom whether or not I should do the show, she said, "Shep, you should have been on TV years ago!"

Unlike Forrest's mom, my mom knew her son's destiny. Despite her enthusiasm, though, I did have to figure it out on my own. I ended up saying yes (obviously), but I definitely had some major hesitation. How can you not listen to and consider the reservations that many of your friends have about a Big Life Decision? The one thing I wanted to know was: Can I somehow walk away if I feel like a shitshow is occurring? The answer was: "Sort of." Basically, I decided that it was worth it, and from the start it turned out to actually be fun. We were off to the races. The only thing we didn't know was how people would react when they watched it, but I remember several times while we were shooting the first season thinking, *This is one funny shitshow.*

So here I am. I followed my destiny from the kid who was crowned Most Enthusiastic in elementary school, on to college, then to business school and Dubai and on to a Charleston rooftop and, eventually, to *Southern Charm*. Or maybe I didn't follow it, maybe I just stumbled around and said yes when opportunity knocked. Because if I'm anything, I'm curious, I'm always up for whatever, and I'm willing to try anything at least once. I guess that's my business plan.

Yes, I used to scoff at reality TV, but you know who else scoffs at reality TV? People who never anted up in life and people who don't "get the joke." What's funny is that I've met a handful of celebrities in the last few years, and the ones who look down their nose at you for being on reality TV are the ones whose career maybe isn't where they want it to be, or they're struggling and a bit insecure. The bigger the "star," the more interested and gracious and curious they are about what it is I do and how everything works (basically "how the sausage is made").

Besides, why should I feel bad about being on a reality show? I never set out to be Daniel Day-Lewis. I just wanted to be Calvin from *Calvin and Hobbes*, and in many ways I'm succeeding.

I've put a lot of thought into the pros and cons of being in a reality show over the years, and after much soulful contemplation, and after meeting all sorts of fans and attending a crazy and wonderful event called BravoCon in the fall of 2019, I've come to this conclusion: We amuse people and take them away for a bit, and that's the only goal of entertainment. People finish work for the day and they have a long commute home, they make dinner for their kids and put them to sleep, and then they turn on Bravo and they're brought into our crazy world for an hour, and it's a much-needed escape.

Did the *Southern Charm* cast all pay our dues toiling away in theater and going on auditions and dealing with rejection and heartbreak in Hollywood? No. We took other paths that were filled with different hardships (well, actually, Shepland has been pretty good). I admit that I was wrong years ago to scoff. It was about me, not the genre. Because being able to give people a release in the form of happiness or heartache or drunken debauchery is an honor. And no more was I aware of this than at BravoCon. The fans were so enthusiastic and happy to see us, I felt like a Beatle (minus the musical talent). There was just support out the wazoo, and it really drove some things home for all of us. Like the fact that we need to appreciate where destiny has taken us because of the fans and support we receive, but also because that place includes guys with black suits holding a sign with our name on it at LaGuardia

Airport, which leads to a Mercedes parked on the curb ready to take us to a hotel suite in Manhattan. It's insane. And don't get me started on all the free clothes.

Admittedly, before *Southern Charm*, I was always calculating how much money I needed and how much (or little) I needed to do in order to just exist (and have some fun, obviously). Is that lack of ambition or total, Buddha-like enlightenment? I guess I never figured I was going to be that guy with the jet and four houses. Nor did I really think that was necessary (although it sounds badass). I'm the guy who, even if he can afford a beach-front property, wants the house one street behind, since the wear and tear of the salt air and the flood insurance are insufferable. I'm also the guy whose cell phone is never under 20 percent but never over 80 percent. When it charges over 80 percent, I feel like I'm overworking the phone and it needs a break. I'm practical and pragmatic if nothing else.

It's a great source of pride that for generations, my family has done very well, and it's covered on the show to a certain extent, but I'm also pretty wary of it. There's a saying that rich screams and wealth whispers, and I was always taught to whisper, so talking about it all is something I'm very allergic to, but here goes. My dad's family has a town named after them here in South Carolina, and they were granted the land by King George II in the late 1700s. My mom's family built the railroads in Chicago (on her mom's side) and her dad's dad played football at Vanderbilt and became a U.S. senator out of Selma, Alabama. I guess one way of putting it is that there's a bit of a cushion that exists for me.

My parents and grandparents were always very careful not to mention it or glorify it. We never had nice cars or garish toys, but we knew the cushion was there. What I tried to figure out along the way was this: What could I do professionally that's respectable but not *too* strenuous so that I could just travel and have fun and be comfortable, and live the life of a benevolent pirate inspired by Hemingway or Jimmy Buffett. Basically, my goals have long been: surf, fish, drink, and laugh. Please don't confuse this with a mantra like "Eat Pray Love" or "Live Laugh Love" or whatever people stitch on pillows. I don't need a "Surf Drink Fish Laugh" pillow unless Craig's company is making it.

The point is, I've been living this way for a long time, and honestly, it just never gets old. Maybe one day I'll wake up (just before noon) and say "Enough!" I wouldn't mind a more sedentary life eventually, but thus far, it hasn't come close to happening. I've also been blessed (or cursed) by the fact that I just don't get hungover. I do love to sleep, so that's my vice after a bender, but I'm ready to go again at a moment's notice. Like I said, it's either a blessing or a curse. I'm going with blessing.

I get a lot of flak on social media from angry people who like to lash out at me, saying things like "You've never worked a day in your life / Your parents bankroll your life / You've never lifted a finger." Insert whatever expletives you like. All of these things are false, as you will soon see. Long before anyone cared enough to assassinate my character via social media, people would say that I was part of the "lucky sperm club," which is funny but definitely not a compliment. Yes, by the wonders of nature, luck, destiny, or whatever you want to call it, I was born into a nice and comfortable situation. It could have been worse, but it's not like I murdered someone or made a pact with the devil. I had it good, but it's not like I grew up on a yacht or got a private jet when I turned sixteen. I wasn't a billionaire like Bruce Wayne, but I might be Batman. No one can prove that I'm not.

I've generally had to work my entire adult life (with varying degrees of success). My parents wouldn't have had it any other way. I'm 100 percent sure I COULD NOT sit on my ass and live a full life forgoing all income. That isn't and never was an option. What's funny to me and my castmates (Craig in particular) is when social media "fans" get on our case about being lazy or not contributing to society. Most of us also have other jobs or projects outside of the show (like Craig and his pillows), so it's not like we're a bunch of freeloaders ruining humanity by appearing on a show about Charleston. As I keep saying, people really need to have a beer, delete the tweet, and get in on the joke. Their lives would be much more enjoyable.

Unfortunately, though, if I'm in a mood, I engage with the trolls and fight back. It's stupid, but it can also be fun. It's not like they're that hard to outsmart. But it's like shouting into an abyss. It's a no-win situation, so I TRY not to engage. I'm only human, though.

As far as contributing to society, I understand that the *Southern Charm* cast isn't out there curing a disease, but like I mentioned before, we entertain/distract people, which is a form of public service. Also, I pay my taxes. I don't harm anyone in society, so what on earth is wrong with what we do or who we are? Would you rather that I had graduated from business school and had gone to work for Goldman Sachs, becoming perversely incentivized to sell toxic assets to your grandparents? What if I was head of marketing for Philip Morris? Would that validate me?

"Celebrities" are always told to shut up and stay in their lane, meaning don't talk about politics or society or anything meaningful, really. I'm a literate, discerning, well-intentioned citizen with full voting rights, so what lane *should* I drive in? This is my fucking lane. Should a cashier also stay in their lane? Retail talk only, dammit!

I happen to have been placed in a good position, and I'm just trying to enjoy the view. Stopping and smelling the roses is a priority for me, and it's a hell of a lot of fun, to boot. Why should I apologize for that?

But just in case you still hate me, here is a list of jobs I've had that will maybe validate my existence in your mind (or maybe they'll make you hate me even more. It's a toss-up):

Sailing instructor / rental associate: I begin with my all-time favorite job. God, I loved it. I was at the end of high school, and one of my best friends and I would meet at the dock on the southern tip of Hilton Head at 8:00 a.m. (the start time was my least favorite part) and the owner of the Commander Zodiac would meet us there. He did dolphin-sighting tours, and he was an avid sailor and a good guy. Every morning we'd teach up to ten kids the basics of sailing a little Sailfish sailboat. The kids were great, and we'd take them over to a barrier island and explore, basically killing a few hours so their parents could explore the bars and restaurants (well, that's what I would do).

In the afternoons we'd sit around, smoke a huge joint, and wait for someone to walk by and ask to go on a tour (hey, I said I've had tons of jobs; I never said they were grueling). Besides, we provided a community service for every girl who walked by, inviting them to parties later that night and giving them an excuse to ditch their parents. One day I spotted a very attractive girl walking along the water, and as I was talking to her, I noticed that her legs were hairier than mine, and at that moment I discovered an important life skill: the importance of being quick on your feet with a lie. When she asked for my number, I changed the final digit *just* as her legs came into focus. Hairy legs were not my thing (still aren't), and I didn't want to waste her time or mine. I can't put that life skill on a résumé, but it does come in handy.

We were all a deep purple shade of tan by the end of the summer. We looked like walking eggplants with white hair. At the end of the summer we went to a Widespread Panic concert and accidentally on purpose ate five hits of acid (each) and somehow ended up locked in a girl's dad's study, where we discovered a book covered in tinfoil called *Fly Fishing Through the Midlife Crisis,* which my friends and I still laugh about to this day. Maybe I should actually read the thing now that I'm in my forties.

Busboy: My mom's full-time job during the summers when I was a teenager was to make sure that I was looking for a job. All I wanted to do was surf, build bike ramps, and play pickup basketball. My mom made all of my meals and I lived at home, so why did I need a job? Every summer I would half-heartedly look for work in June. I'd turn in a few résumés, go back to playing basketball, and by July my mom would usually have given up on me, helplessly watching me and my pothead friends do backflips on BMX bikes into our pool. I'm sure it was very pleasant and relaxing for her. One summer, probably to spare herself three months of anxiety, she made sure to secure a job for me at her friend's restaurant Truffles, as a busboy. It wasn't ideal for me, since I usually create messes, not fix them. The one thing I did like about the job was the bread and Boursin cheese they served. That Boursin was like crack to me, so you could usually find me in the kitchen with the dishwashers munching on bread and cheese, trying to make solid weed connections. As you can probably guess, I was unceremoniously "let go," and I happily went back to terrorizing the neighborhood and organizing parties. Well, not organizing per se (too much effort), but attending parties for sure.

Pizza deliverer: When I was nineteen years old, I came home from college for the summer, and this time I actually *had* to get a job. Since I wasn't a high schooler being supported by Mom and Dad, money started to become a necessity for staples like beer and the various things you need to score chicks (drinks, dinners, the occasional game of pool, mushroom tea, corsages, Ping-Pong balls, laughing gas, yo-yos, parachutes, neck braces, etc.). A guy a little older than me was running a pizza place called Davinci's Pizza, and he liked me, so he hired me as a delivery boy. I liked this job. I'd drive around and make people happy by bringing them food. That was the job description. I worked from 6:00 p.m. until 10:00 p.m., and when I met up with my buddies I had about sixty bucks in my pocket. The problem was that I would always forget to check the order, so I would forget a two-liter Sprite or some extra breadsticks, and customers would get pissed. A man can't master every profession, though, so I give myself a solid 6 for this one.

Expeditor: This is the job that redeemed me! It was at the Mangy Moose restaurant in Jackson Hole, Wyoming. The Moose is actually a famous steak joint and music venue at the base of Teton Village. I lived in Jackson Hole for a summer, and the manager who hired me was cool, and passionate about the job. The chef and the kitchen staff were all kayakers and fishermen; they were relaxed but serious about their work. After a few weeks they decided to trust me and give me the job of expeditor, which meant that I made sure all the meals got out to the right tables on time. If *I* screwed up, it screwed *everything* up. I liked and respected these guys, and I dared not let them down, so I took the position very seriously. They gave me a hard time because I was a little college boy, but I eventually earned their respect. At least, I think I did, since they let me smoke a joint with them at the end of each shift. During that summer, I burned my arm so many times carrying so many piping-hot steak plates into the dining room, to the point that I became calloused and impervious to the pain. I guess you could call that another on-the-job life skill for my résumé. I healed quickly, though. My hands basically look like they've been soaking in Ivory since I was born. Manual labor is not my strong suit.

Surf instructor (sort of): This was my first job out of college, working for a fun forty-something-year-old guy in Charleston who had a small real estate business. The problem was that he was going through a divorce and he had three kids, ages eleven, ten, and eight. Right when I got hired, his ex-wife got engaged to another man, and my boss got custody of the kids the week after I started working for him. Essentially, I was his fourth kid. He had no time to run a business since he was Mr. Mom all of a sudden. I loved it, though. I wasn't making much money, but he'd call me on my way into work and say, "Change of plans: you're taking my son surfing today!" Hell yeah. My dream job. Those kids were great, and my first (rather unproductive) job out of college was a true success (except financially, I guess). Side note: Instead of gaining the "freshman fifteen" during the school year, I gained weight after the year was up. On the way to my job, I would grab a blueberry muffin and a Cherry Coke for breakfast, then a bowl of chili, turkey sandwich, and fries for lunch, and then, for a sensible dinner, I'd have a six-pack of beer. I knew I was getting chubby when the buttons on my pants started to fly across the room every time I sat down, thus becoming dangerous projectiles.

Secret shopper: After several years of fruitless postcollege professional pursuits in Charleston, my dad insisted I get my shit together and get a real job—one with a boss who asked me to do something besides take his kids surfing. I didn't want to disappoint my dad, so I got a job down in West Palm Beach with the home-building giant Pulte Homes. I didn't hate it; it was corporate and a bit stifling at times, but there were also some really cool guys in the upper positions, and they enjoyed my watercooler stories about babes and beers. My job was to be a "secret shopper" and go around finding out how competitors were doing in our market, and around Florida. I was on the road a lot, and it was like I was a pizza delivery boy all over again, mixed with a secret agent. There were two schools of thought about how to do this job. One was to just go in, say you work for a competitor, and ask how they were doing. The problem was, you never knew how honest they'd be, plus it wasn't all that fun. The second school of thought was more my style: Pretend like you're a buyer (even though I was twenty-four years old and looked eighteen), make up a story about who you are, and try to do some math in your head and figure out how quickly the community is selling homes and what types of homes; essentially so we can copy what they're doing, or if it's not performing well, learn from their mistakes. Creating a secret identity was my favorite part of the job, although I wasn't always great at it. Once, I got lazy, and when the competitor's salesperson approached me, I said, "I'm looking for my parents." What I meant was that I was looking for a home for my parents, but I guess I really did look young, because, totally deadpan, they replied: "Where's the last place you saw them?" All I could do in that moment was admit I was a spy. The job had other perks, like giving me the chance to meet women in faraway places. One time in Naples, Florida, I had dinner at the bar of an Outback Steakhouse. The bartender was hot, and every douche sitting near me was drooling. I made a few offhand funny comments and left my number on the bottom of my check and wrote "call me." Wouldn't you know it, she called! I told her to bring a case of beer to the Ramada Inn where I was staying, and oh, what a night we had! At the end of my tenure as a secret agent I sort of screwed up, though. I went to a conference in Orlando and was just dead tired from the Ramada experience (thank you, Outback, "No Rules, Just Right," indeed!). I couldn't keep my eyes open, so I nodded off a few times at the conference and got put on "double-secret-probation" by a woman who I'm pretty sure didn't like me and my carefree attitude, even though the older guys at the company thought I was hilarious. She had a job to do, I guess, so I sheepishly accepted the punishment, whatever the fuck "double-secret-probation" meant.

Market analyst: Eventually, I knew I had to leave the Pulte job. It was boring, and I was starting to treat it as such (for example, by falling asleep at conferences). Plus, I was in my mid-twenties, and all the new guys coming into the office taking all the cool positions had gone to grad school and were telling me that in a big corporate environment like this you couldn't get anywhere without a business degree. I had been living in my grandparents' house in Florida (they were only there two months of the year), and they told me that the famous golfer Greg Norman was speaking at their country club and asked if I wanted to join them. I was a huge fan of his, so I said sure. There I was, listening to his life story, and I especially took interest in all the business success he had achieved. Then and there, I devised a plan: I was going to ask Greg Norman if I could get a job with his organization, Medallist Developments. I told my grandparents that I would meet them at home, and I waited in line to say hello to Mr. Norman. He was very nice, and I manned up and asked him for a job.

He passed me off to his business partner, Bart, and I was off to the races. Sort of. It took about four months of clandestine back-and-forth communication (so no one at my Pulte job would find out), but I finally got the job! I can't tell you how good it feels to work behind the scenes and lock down another gig when you aren't loving your current one. But I'd be remiss if I didn't mention *part* of the reason I got my new job with Medallist Developments. When I interviewed with the president of the company (I'll call him Edward), he asked where I was from. I said I was from South Carolina, and so was he! Then he said, "Wait, is your mom Frances Hobbs?" I told him that was her maiden name, and then Edward said he went out on a date with my mom when they were in college in Chapel Hill. No fucking way! Needless to say, the interview went well.

When I got to the parking lot after the interview, I immediately called my mom and told her about Edward. She said, "I remember Edward. He got arrested during our date for jumping on a cop car, and we had to bail him out of jail." At that moment I thought, *Hot damn, this is the job for me!* I worked in market analysis and land acquisitions for two years for Medallist. It was an Australian company, and I met some great Aussies (I swear I'm part Australian). I was loving life, but eventually I decided it was time to heed the advice of my older friends at Pulte and start thinking about business school.

· CHAPTER 3 ·

LOSING IT

I was a precocious and tempestuous young whippersnapper, and I've had my fair share of adventures when it comes to working (or not working), but there's a major force that helped to shape me into the man I am today that I haven't yet spoken about, and that force is called . . . puberty.

Or, as some would say, one's "formative years."

Many of my "formative years" were spent at boarding school, until I was kicked out my senior year, five months before graduation. As I write this book, I'm on an email chain with some of my former classmates who are planning a reunion, and it's taking every bit of self-control I possess (which isn't a ton) not to hit Reply All and write *F*CK YOU!* My classmates didn't have the final power to kick me out, but some of them shoved me toward the door. It all worked out in the end, but at the time it felt apocalyptic. I guess it still does, since I still feel the urge to email profanities to them in all caps. Restraint hasn't always been my strong suit.

So how did a model citizen like myself wind up at boarding school? It's not for the reasons you might think. My older sister is and was the smartest person in our family. She had her nose in a book her entire childhood. I remember being gobsmacked that she didn't like spending the night at friends' houses when we were kids because she would rather be home reading. Are you kidding me?! For me, spending the night with friends felt like a giant safari into the unknown, the only true pitfall being whenever I wound up at a house where the mom was "healthy" and had an awful snack cabinet. When saltine crackers and ice water are the highlights, you know you're in trouble.

I'm proud to say that the snack cupboard at the Rose residence was robust and bountiful! Shark Bites fruit snacks, Gushers, Oreos, Girl Scout Cookies—we had it all. Rounding out the bounty, my mom made and still makes the best grilled cheese on the planet (her "secret" is Velveeta singles). In the morning, the sweet, sweet morning, she made all-you-can-eat chocolate chip pancakes. We had kids lined up around the block to be granted the rights of a Rose sleepover! So, maybe it isn't so weird that my sister didn't want to leave our house. But I digress . . .

As I said, my sister was extremely smart, and my mom decided that she needed to leave Hilton Head to seek a top-notch education at a boarding school up north somewhere. My sister and my mom visited them all: Deerfield, Hotchkiss, Choate, Exeter—you get the idea. They ended up liking a school in northern Virginia called Episcopal High School the most, a beautiful and historic school outside Washington, D.C. The school had just become coed and (one could argue) northern Virginia is Southern (I guess it depends on which side of the Mason-Dixon Line you're standing on). It was beautiful: rolling green hills and old brick buildings, just like in the movies. All of the students were boarders, even if they lived nearby, and most of the faculty lived on campus, literally down the hall from us. What could go wrong? My sister was unsurprisingly doing very well there, so when it came time for me to go off to school and "broaden my horizons," I just followed her lead.

Even though I might seem pissed about getting kicked out of the school, I'm not bitter. Not 100 percent. I forged some lifelong relationships there, and the education I received was second to none and highly competitive. We read and studied Chaucer and Shakespeare, and we even delved into Tom Stoppard's *Rosencrantz and Guildenstern Are Dead*, which is a somewhat satirical and cool play about two minor characters from *Hamlet*, similar to Samuel Beckett's *Waiting for Godot* (which we also read). It was around this time that literature became interesting and fun to me. Before boarding school, there was always a boring list of books that everyone had to read over the summer or in class, and it was mostly Steinbeck's *The Pearl*, Hemingway's *The Old Man and the Sea* (which won him the Pulitzer Prize, but I think it's one of his most boring works), and the all-time worst book in the history of civilization: Stephen Crane's *The Red Badge of Courage*. My mom and I almost killed each other every summer because of these required books, because I never wanted to sit still long enough to read a stream-of-consciousness book about the Civil War or some stupid pearl. I wanted to play sports or shoot alligators with BB guns.

That all changed thanks to boarding school. Somehow, I was suddenly happy to trade in the BB guns for time spent sitting in a classroom breaking down characters and themes in Shakespeare's plays. It was like a light bulb going off in my brain. My love of literature also eventually helped me get girls, but I'll get to that later.

During this time, I especially loved Polonius's advice to his son Laertes in *Hamlet*, before Laertes heads off to school. Not all of Polonius's advice was golden, but this one is a gem:

Be thou familiar, but by no means vulgar:
Those friends thou hast, and their adoption tried,
Grapple them unto thy soul with hoops of steel;
But do not dull thy palm with entertainment
Of each new-hatch'd, unfleg'd comrade.

Not that I astutely followed much of this advice, but it just made me nostalgic for all the well-intentioned guidance I got from loved ones before I left for school. I've always loved the saying "Do as I say, not as I do." There are some really useful nuggets in the quote. Polonius talks about not being gaudy and flashy (lessons I learned from generations of my family that I wholeheartedly agree with). Also, don't borrow or lend money—a lesson we all must learn over time, especially when friendships are involved. And perhaps the most famous lines of advice in literary history, "To thine own self be true!" Never try to be someone you are not.

I loved digging into these famous texts and discovering that Shakespeare had invented stories and themes that writers have been mimicking in one way or another for hundreds of years (like this book, if it were written in iambic pentameter). My favorite play of all was *Henry IV, Part 1* and *2*. No surprise: This is where a precocious and fun-loving Prince Hal parties and carries on with a group of fun-loving ne'er-do-wells (I guess you can say I aspired to be him). In *Part 2*, he has to make a decision about whether to grow up and take the reins from his father as king, ditching his rapscallion friends, led by his mentor, the prodigious partier and joie de vivre proponent Falstaff. God, I loved Falstaff and all the promises of a good time that he embodied. Of course, Hal, who I also loved, makes the difficult and mature decision to leave his degenerate friends behind—a decision that I would not and have not made. But let's face it, I have considerably less at stake. It's not like wars will break out if I don't change my ways. Hal had a raw deal in that sense.

I would compare some of my boarding school friendships to the closeness that WWII soldiers felt when they were trapped behind enemy lines with danger around every corner. Most of the faculty was like the secret police, and I'm only exaggerating a little here. Whenever we were away for the weekend (after filling out the proper permission slips and forms), the dean of students would go into full detective mode and put the pieces of a puzzle together so he could bust us for drinking beers at a friend's house who lived nearby. It was a constant game of cat and mouse, and it was so unnecessary. Didn't the dean have a life? Why did he care what we did on our off time? Did he think he was responsible for the lives of minors or something? Okay, fine . . . on that score, I guess he was.

What made the faculty most like the secret police was that the bust never ended with one person getting in trouble. It was always an interrogation, like: "We know it's not your fault, but whose fault is it? Who was with you? We'll lighten your punishment if you cooperate."

We were teenagers getting treated like FBI informants, with promises of clemency. The honor code at the school said you must not cheat, but if you discover someone cheating and you don't turn them in, you yourself are breaking the honor code! If you've seen *Dead Poets Society* with Robin Williams, it was exactly like that, rules-wise and aesthetically: rolling hills, lush forest, and humorless administrators who were definitely not in on the joke.

In my school, it felt like there were spies everywhere, and just my luck, I had landed in the class with the most spies. I will eventually get to the actual reason I was kicked out, but you need to hear my full side of the story to understand that I was completely innocent. Or marginally innocent. I often wonder, why couldn't I have landed in my sister's class, which was full of hilarious and irreverent students who were always having fun and being slightly subversive? I basically learned everything I know and became the man I am today by hanging out with the older kids. We'd eat acid and smoke dope in the dorm and just laugh the night away, while the kids in my class were probably busy peeking around corners, taking notes on our whereabouts, and trying to bug our room so they could play the tape for the dean. We learned a lot about ourselves mentally in those days, and in addition to my love of literature, boarding school also awakened my lust, and I owe one of my first (semi) sexual experiences to a local girl who was somewhat of a legend, nicknamed Snake Boots.

One night, the older guys said they had a rite of passage for me (or, as some may say, they wanted to haze me). The plan was to get me drunk and sneak Snake Boots into the dorm. I suspect her name came from the fact that she would allegedly undertake an arduous journey scaling the campus fences and crossing frozen tundra to get to our dorm, and she wore boots to do it. Who knows? In any case, they told me she loved to indoctrinate young men who needed a little extra shove to get to legendary status. Translation: I was a skinny, awkward virgin, and they told me Snake Boots could help rid me of that blight.

I wish I could say I had some luck with Snake Boots, but I'd be lying, and I promise to you, dear reader, that everything in this book is true. I was the perfect candidate, though: goofy and slightly pathetic, with a tinge of potential. I was definitely a late bloomer. At that time, I thought of girls as this magnificent and mysterious meta-species, almost like a deity. I was never quite sure why they would ever be interested in guys. I've always loved the *Seinfeld* quote from Elaine: "The female body is a work of art. The male body is utilitarian—it's for getting around. It's like a Jeep." I agree. If I could only go back in time knowing what I know now: that girls were just as insecure and awkward as we were back then.

I was never smooth. I was tall, grossly skinny, bird-chested . . . I was basically the captain of the weird-body team. And sadly, my run-in with Snake Boots didn't cure me.

Alas, I woke up the next afternoon and everyone in the dorm was laughing that I had blown it with Snake Boots. My life at that moment felt like a 1980s teen comedy, and I was the butt of the joke. Snake Boots tried to have her way with me, but because I had zero alcohol tolerance (I was skinny and bird-chested, remember), I just passed out cold. I wasn't even mad, though. I feel proud to have been part of such a calamitous adventure, and maybe even a little happy that I later ended up losing my virginity card to someone I actually loved. Or liked a lot. Or like-loved? Anyway, I'll call her Jenny, and she was great.

Before Jenny I was definitely in no-man's-land romantically. I remember friends making out with girls in seventh grade on the playground during varsity basketball games, and I was uninterested and couldn't believe that they'd want to miss the game for a girl. I was addicted to basketball and surfing, and everything else took a backseat. My first kiss was in eighth grade with a girl called Tina who went to the public school on Hilton Head (it's a small island), and it happened right after I went surfing at night with some friends. It was a full moon, and I remember being sort of scared I was going to get eaten by a shark because I'd heard they feed at night. I came in from the water, and there were girls on the beach, and Tina and I went to this bench on a golf course overlooking a pond and . . . we kissed! She definitely made the first move, but since everyone else I knew was already making out, I got off the sidelines and into the game. We shared a big, sloppy French kiss that I later described to my best friend as being akin to standing in a waterfall—that's how wet and sloppy it was. But dammit I had done it. I was off the bench and driving to the hoop.

It was good to get it out of the way, but I can't say I was eager to spend the evening swapping buckets of spit with girls after that kiss. I just wanted to surf and shoot hoops. Tina had other ideas, though. She started to write our names together in all sorts of artful and creative ways on her school binder. Apparently, she was already planning our wedding. This sort of irrational exuberance forced me to emotionally withdraw from her. My binder was full of drawings of athletes like Michael Jordan and Kelly Slater. I didn't have room left to draw Tina's name, literally or emotionally. I took a sabbatical from the crazy little thing called love for a while. I let my friends do the exploring, and then they dutifully reported back to me. I didn't give them any competition whatsoever. You're welcome, guys!

Then, in the blink of an eye, everything changed.

One fateful day in the ninth grade, I saw two girls playfully wrestling in the lounge area at school, and I got all warm and fuzzy—and that was it for me. Suddenly basketball and surfing took a backseat. You may notice the rather large gap from this moment until I actually lost my V-card senior year of high school. Let me again remind you of the awkward years: I looked like *Sesame Street*'s Big Bird with a chest so skinny it looked inverted. I liked girls, I wanted them, but I couldn't fathom how or why they'd like me. I was just a goofy and hyper little teenager with no moves whatso-ever. It also didn't help that I always liked popular older girls, since they were just absolutely unattainable. I remember there was one girl who I'd call on the phone, and I would have a script all written out with questions I'd ask plus possible answers from her, which would lead to a series of follow-up questions depending upon her answer. It was like a choose-your-own-adventure book.

In boarding school, I eventually grew out of the awkward phase, and by senior year I had filled out a little (probably from having the munchies 24/7). I had been a sailing instructor at Commander Zodiac (remember, the best job ever), had a nice tan and long hair tucked behind my ears. I was improving. I had the confidence to maybe think girls might actually be interested in me. After all, my friends and I were suddenly the cool seniors of the school and we had all the weed, we knew where to score beers, we organized the parties, and so of course the girls were into that. Plus, I was the singer in a Grateful Dead cover band, so that didn't hurt. I did a scorching rendition of "China Cat Sunflower" straight into "I Know You Rider" that people still talk about in the halls today, if by "the halls" you're talking about my house in Charleston and by "people" you mean me.

Jenny was a sophomore when I was a senior, and on the dating front I outdid myself convincing her to be my girlfriend and then eventually take my virginity. To this day I'm amazed when guys say they lost their virginity at fourteen or fifteen years old. At that age, I would have fainted if a girl took her clothes off in front of me. By the time I met Jenny, though, I'd gotten over my fear of fainting and was ready to redeem myself after my Snake Boots incident.

Jenny was great, and her parents approved of me because she told them how much I loved books and how great my vocabulary was, so my love of literature came in pretty handy. I remember exactly where we were the first time that we had sex, and I remember the conversation right before it, and the conversation twenty seconds later, when it was finished.

The worst part of being kicked out of boarding school (other than the disappointment of my parents) was that I had to leave Jenny, my first love and girlfriend. It was super sad to leave, and we continued to see each other throughout the summer, but let's face it—the college-bound senior and the girl back at high school combo rarely works (if you don't believe me, just watch the movie *Can't Buy Me Love*). I'm still friendly with Jenny and think the world of her. In fact, I ran into her last summer in the North Carolina mountains at a barbecue restaurant, and we hadn't seen each other in ages. We got to catch up for a little bit, and it made me smile to see that she looked great and seemed to be doing well. She had just camped out in the Appalachians for a few days, so I'm pretty sure we were not destined to be together. Despite the fact that I like to go to my family's farm and hunt and fish, I'm an indoorsman. I can handle maybe one night in a tent with no showers, down pillows, or plumbing, but several? Hell no. If there are huge trout to be caught, or waves to be ridden . . . there are lodges for that, with good food and wine and beds. Sorry, Jenny. We were not meant to be.

The people who dropped the guillotine on me were some of my classmates on the discipline committee. Like I said, we had to have had the nerdiest class in the history of the school. There were like six cool people and the rest were just go-getters and Dudley Do-Rights. You know the type. Self-righteous overachievers who are to be avoided at all costs because they do not get the joke. They were probably organizing Run for the Cure for Acne charity races on the weekends. My friends and I were the ones in the woods smoking and doing the important work of discovering new hookup spots around campus. Those hookup spots were a valuable commodity because every night after study hall the boys and girls would get together, and if you were seeing someone, you'd grab each other and scour the campus for a private place to clumsily make out. Like I said, important work.

Among our discoveries were the gazebo (a popular destination), the squash courts (for pros only), the science lab, and the darkroom (for film development AND make-out sessions). I also once experienced hookup nirvana when I broke into the gym and used the high-jump mat! What a revelation. Basically, my friends and I were the wild Delta Tau Chi frat in the movie *Animal House* and everyone else was the nerdy buttoned-up fraternity and sorority. I was actually kicked out due to an accumulation of offenses, small things that just added up, like drinking, smoking pot, bending rules—enjoying life, basically.

So to sum up, I got kicked out and had to leave Jenny behind because I had too much fun at boarding school. My poor parents (this is a recurring theme in my life, so sorry, Mom . . . again).

As a proud boarding school nongraduate, I say that if any parent or administrator is thinking of touting boarding school, I'd think again. You take a bunch of hormonal kids from all over the country and mix them together, and then tell them to not break the ten thousand rules that you set. Meanwhile, back home all your friends just got their first car, they're throwing beer bashes and having actual bedrooms to get busy in. I was kicked out mostly for just trying to get away with doing the things my friends back home did all the time, only they didn't have self-appointed police watching their every move. Even though it sucked in the moment, once again the magic of Shepland took hold, and I was able to finish high school back home, so it all worked out.

I didn't know it at the time, but getting kicked out of boarding school would eventually help me land at a college where there were *plenty* of girls, as opposed to a college in the mountains with approximately two girls. Here's what happened: Based on my good grades and SAT scores (yes, you read that right) I had gotten an early acceptance to Sewanee: The University of the South, in the mountains of Tennessee. It's a cool little liberal arts college, but it's most definitely a small pond. I was pretty excited to go there at first; it was college, after all, and you could drink beer without being hunted down and tortured (or kicked out). That said, I did foresee a bit of a problem: It was a small town in the mountains with just fifteen hundred students, so to me it sounded a little like the sequel to boarding school.

When I was kicked out of boarding school, Sewanee said that they would no longer be honoring their early admittance, making the tail-between-my-legs journey back home to Hilton Head even more arduous and fraught with peril. My dad was pretty upset, understandably. But you know what, the experience was also a testament to how lucky I am to have such great parents. They actually felt bad for me. Yes, they voiced their disappointment, but they also knew how badly I was hurting and how devastated I was. I was seventeen years old, and this was a pivotal point in my life, emotionally and otherwise. They made sure that I was going to right the ship and get through this rough patch, and it really did and does mean the world to me that they cared so much.

So once I got back home, the game plan was to get a college advisor and figure out what my next move was. It was March of my senior year, so pretty late in the game college admissions–wise, and we had to move quickly. I volunteered at the Boys & Girls Club of Hilton Head Island, mainly hanging out with the kids and playing basketball. I once dunked on a ten-year-old kid and became a minor celebrity in their eyes for about four minutes. My "dunk heard around the southeast" got me only so far. After that, I was furiously applying to schools, and I got some interest from the University of Georgia. After all, I did have a decent résumé and test scores, so if you just turned a blind eye to the whole kicked-out-of-school thing, I looked like a pretty good candidate. I got in, and the rest is history. I wound up in Athens, the greatest college town in America, with a huge football program and as many lovely girls as any one straight dude could ever hope to be surrounded by. Eureka! I'm fairly certain I would have burned all meaningful sexual bridges at Sewanee in less than a year. Now I was a medium-size fish in a very big pond. I had plenty of room to eat, grow, swim, and misbehave! (Note to Craig: New pillow alert!)

So here we go again. Back to Forrest Gump's mom and her speech about destiny. Does everything happen for a reason? Was getting kicked out of boarding school the best thing for me? Or am I fairly adroit (with the loving support of family) at turning lemons into lemonade? I would like to say that if anyone at the Episcopal High School endowment office is reading this, please stop asking me for financial contributions. (Yes, they still want a check from me!) While I appreciate the chutzpah, and fondly remember a handful of professors and am forever grateful for being introduced to Tom Stoppard's work, please consider this chapter an official "unsubscribe" from your donation list. Ask one of the Dudley Do-Rights from my class; I'm sure they would rather spend their money on your fine institution than on beer and surf trips to Tahiti, unlike me.

So there you have it—I lost my virginity at boarding school, me, a late bloomer with a bird chest. I'd almost argue that not much changed in my twenties and thirties, except instead of a bird chest there's a little beer belly to contend with. I'm still captain of the weird-body team! To be honest, I've never once thought of myself as an attractive dude. I don't use hair products or dress nice (except for when I have to, like the occasional wedding or event). All I've ever wanted was to laugh and make others laugh. It sounds cliché and like a self-help declaration, but I swear it's true. I never really had "moves." But I have donned a neck brace and done fake falls in front of a bunch of hot girls to get their attention (it worked).

Despite what some might think, I don't consider myself all that smooth. I have never been a whisper-sweet-little-nothings kind of guy. As noncommittal and flippant as I might be, I take pride in the fact that I do not make promises I can't keep to get laid. I don't promise the moon and the stars while my eye is wandering to another girl across the room—and a big fuck off to those who do! I've always maintained that I just like to have fun, and a big part of having fun is being with girls. It turns out that the Cyndi Lauper song "Girls Just Want to Have Fun" is true (although my favorites are "Time After Time" and "True Colors"). If you show a girl a good time, whether it be on a boat, at a ball game, playing beer pong, or fake tripping while wearing a neck brace, if you make them laugh, you will get girls. It's not that complicated. You also absolutely, positively have to have a sense of humor about yourself—that's a must. Create a fun, light environment and you're "in like Flynn."

Another important rule when it comes to women is to never act aggressive. Act like a gentleman (as much as you can after twelve beers), stay relaxed, don't try too hard, and maybe just steal a kiss here and there. I had a friend who took a really beautiful girl out four times and they had a blast, but he never tried anything. After the fourth date, she attacked him, and they had sex in his car! I love that. Anticipation can be maddening and intoxicating.

Being a lot of fun mixed with being respectful is a winning combination. If you aren't that gregarious, you can be the silent, brooding type in the corner. It's a role I'm incapable of playing—except for once, by accident. I was with friends, partying hard, and we took a flight on Singapore Air from Thailand to Bali to surf. On the flight I was fresh out of serotonin: joyless and brooding. The flight attendants were all hot, so my friends were chatting them up, but I was all out of charm. The next night we ran into the flight attendants at a pool party, and one of them told my buddy that she liked me on the plane because I seemed dark and disturbed. Me! The Emperor of Shepland! My friends almost passed out laughing. The bewildered girls asked what was so funny, and my friends pointed over at me, and there I was, in the pool with a local babe on my shoulders, engaged in an epic game of chicken fight with another couple. Her dreams of the brooding guy in the corner were shattered.

I have some good insight about getting girls, but once you get the girl? I still haven't figured this out. I'll paraphrase the OutKast song "Hey Ya!" to get my point across more poetically:

Know what they say is
Nothing lasts forever!

I've thought about this often, why monogamy and relationships don't work (at least for me so far). Very few species mate for life (penguins, beavers, wolves, gibbons . . .) And they may mate for life, but they don't get married (for obvious reasons, but still). Marriage was a concept created when the average life expectancy was like twenty-five years old, in order to ensure that two people procreated and took care of children so they could grow up and propagate the species. What about lust, though? That's a powerful emotion. Should we bury it forever once we are in a relationship? Yes, you can lust after a spouse, but come on.

The weird thing is that my parents have been married for close to fifty years, and there's been almost no divorce in my extended family. I have all the good, solid relationship examples one could seek. But for some reason I just get pessimistic when it comes to marriage and commitment. Or is it realistic? When it comes to relationships, I guess I'm still a late bloomer. And maybe that's my Forrest Gump destiny. All I know is that if I had married a girlfriend years ago and had kids and a "normal" job, you wouldn't be reading this. You'd probably be slogging through *The Brothers Karamazov* by Fyodor Dostoevsky or something equally dense instead . . . so, you know, you're welcome.

· CHAPTER 4 ·

THE TOOTH HURTS

This chapter is going to be full of painful memories, or memories of physical pain. Either way, it will change your life. Or entertain you. Or make you squirm. Here goes . . .

Let's start with the facts:

I have had stitches *in my head alone* over ten times. In case you're reading this drunk and you're confused, that's not ten stitches in my head one time, that's many stitches in various parts of my head ten different times. And in case you're sober and doubting me, I consulted with my personal historian (aka my mom) and she confirmed the numbers, and by her account ten might actually be a conservative number. But let's go with ten.

I have also broken both feet and hands several times, and I've had teeth knocked out on multiple occasions, as you will see.

But why, you might wonder, am I telling you about all of my physical injuries as if I'm a decorated soldier or an MMA champ? A couple reasons:

A. I figure I'm lucky to be alive, a hundred times over. And that realization has informed my decision-making as I've grown older. My injuries have given me a "seize the day" attitude, which leads to me taking chances and doing things that more conservative people with fewer stitches in their personal history might scoff at.

B. I'm starting to think that today's kids are completely coddled and overprotected, to their detriment. Assessing risk and personal limits is essential. Throwing caution to the wind is also sometimes important, even if it's only to help you realize you don't have the stomach (or pain threshold) for it. So maybe this will inspire parents to loosen the reins a little? Your kids don't have to have ten head wounds to live a happy life, but a stitch here and there? Let them live a little.

Despite what it sounds like, I wasn't even the wildest SOB on the block. There were a handful of other kids who would engage in extremely risky and psychotic behavior, like doing backflips into pools *from the roof*, stealing bikes, or waterskiing in a gator-infested lagoon while being pulled from a moving car on the shore. I confess I did burn ants with a magnifying glass once (sorry, PETA). Maybe I fell out of trees, but other kids shot BB guns at each other! Actually, I also did this. Often.

Still, my buddies and I knew, somewhere in the back of our adolescent minds, that we had a lot to lose and that torching bridges (or ants) and accruing a dangerous reputation was not gonna be good for business long term. There were plenty of kids I grew up with who didn't mind truly breaking the rules, and some of them wound up robbing banks and selling drugs (one guy I knew wound up working as a cable guy by day and he sold drugs at night—that is, before he got caught). I was right on the cusp of following in those footsteps, but I never veered over to the dark side for very long, mostly because of my parents. Because of them, I knew what the stakes were if I screwed up, and they taught us right from wrong from an early age. I was more like an instigator or catalyst for wild and potentially dangerous ideas, like Woody Woodpecker. Mild insanity and chaos followed in my wake. I definitely didn't play it safe, but I was often rescued or I happened to fall on the right side of the cliff. Whether that was due to blind luck/fate or me in the back of my mind knowing that to besmirch my mother and father's name would be devastating, I can't say for sure. But I was a capricious youth, which in turn led to some trouble—often ending with those damn stitches.

The strangest thing is that over time, all of my wildness and my injuries made me a somewhat cautious person. I came to realize how many times I had barely skated through potentially fatal or crippling disasters, and that realization changed me. You won't find me riding on a motorcycle or heli-skiing. I surf, but not when the waves are over a certain size. I feel like I've tempted fate way too many times, so I quit being reckless. If I ever have a child, I'll tell them, "There are lots of ways to get attention or make someone laugh, and putting yourself in danger of physical harm is definitely a popular one, but please consider the consequences: The end of life as you know it." I would also add, "There is no better way to get attention or affection than by using your wit. Don't be Evel Knievel; be the court jester, hilariously describing the dangerous jump over the Grand Canyon instead." That's my parenting advice: Be funny, and don't get injured.

But back to my injuries. Let's start with the open wounds. The first was when my sister pulled me off the kitchen counter when I was a toddler (I still have the scar under my chin). I got her back a few years later when I pulled the gutter off the roof and it landed on her head, giving her eight stitches over her eye. There was also the BMX bike ramp into our family pool that I'm lucky didn't kill us all. I did a backflip off the ramp and hit my head on the bricks on the side of the pool and, you guessed it, stitches. Then there was the time I was skateboarding in the neighborhood and tried something stupid (like attempting a trick I wasn't remotely qualified to try) and BAM! More stitches. After this skateboard incident the doctors in the hospital put me in a secluded room because they saw how long my injury rap sheet was and they figured I might be a victim of child abuse. It turns out it was the other way around (again, sorry, Mom). Two of my best stitches stories, though, involve Love and the Old West.

Let's start with the Old West. When I was a junior in college in Georgia, I planned a debaucherous manifest destiny road trip to Jackson Hole, Wyoming, with two of my best friends, Andrew and Jim. For some reason we decided to drive across the country in two cars, for three people, which shows you how solid our decision-making was at that time. Andrew's car was nicknamed "the Grave Digger." Another warning sign. It was a ridiculous monster truck–type vehicle with huge wheels and a crappy engine, despite several attempts to rebuild the engine (which actually might explain why it was so shitty). I was in the other car with Jim, which was a hand-me-down from my mom nicknamed "the Blueberry" because of its blue exterior AND blue leather interior. I inherited this car at fifteen, because my parents are the king and queen of hand-me-down cars. We drive them until the wheels fall off, and I'm very proud of this fact. Keeping up with the Joneses and having fancy cars was always scoffed at by my parents. In any case, I drove the Blueberry and we spent twelve days driving across the country (a trip that usually takes three days, FYI).

I wish I could blame the Grave Digger's sketchy engine for our lengthy travel time, but really it was because we decided it would be a good use of our time to stop in cities that had the best classic rock stations. Kansas City hooked us with "Radar Love" by Golden Earring. St. Louis played a mean "Little Wing" by Stevie Ray Vaughan (a killer Hendrix instrumental cover)—you get the idea. So, we stopped at those places and spent the night and tried to find a good time. This was before Tripadvisor and Yelp, so we usually failed in our quest and ended up at a terrible bar on the outskirts of some suburb drinking shots and getting into arguments about who Jim was going to ride with the next day, me or Andrew. Call us a ship of fools or maybe a gang that couldn't shoot straight? The Three Stooges? How about the Keystone Cops? All of these descriptions were applicable. We ended up stopping in Cheyenne, Wyoming, when we easily could have pushed through to Jackson Hole. Cheyenne just had an air of Old West nostalgia, and we wanted to see some real cowboys. I think we actually thought there'd be tumbleweeds rolling down the street.

We finally made it to Jackson Hole and checked into a hotel, sharing a double room with a rollaway bed. Then we got absolutely rip-roaring drunk to celebrate the end of our journey. This was right around the time that the movie *Fight Club* had come out, to give you some context. We get back to the room and decide to beat each other up, *Fight Club*–style. None of us are fighters, at all. But there we were, merrily punching each other. Suddenly, Andrew and I look at each other and decide Jim deserves a beating. He's been like the pretty girl at the dance this whole trip and we've had enough of kissing his ass just so we can have someone to talk to in the car. So we jump him and start whaling on him. He manages to squirm out of our clutches, and he grabs a luggage rack and hits me squarely between the eyes. Blood everywhere! You may be horrified, but we thought it was highly entertaining at the time.

Luckily the hospital was across the street from our shitty motel, and Jim and Andrew gingerly escorted me to the emergency room to get stitched up. The doctor asked what happened and we told him that we were jumped by a bunch of cowboys. We launched into a wild story that involved a girl, some whiskey, and assless chaps. The medical staff asked if they should call the cops, and we demurred and said we were probably asking for the beating. They naively let my friends stay in the room while I got stitched up, but after hearing Andrew and Jim keep saying "You missed a spot," the doctor kicked them out. I suffered ten stitches between my eyes, but I had never laughed so hard under such duress and pain, and I have the Old West to thank for that.

Now let's delve into the Love portion of my Top Stitches of All Time (everyone has a personal-injury list like this, right? No? Just me?). I had just moved to Charleston after college and started working for Exit Realty. I was really into this girl Molly. She had gone to college with some of my friends in Virginia, and so we knew of each other. The problem was that she was sort of seeing someone else, so I was trying to figure out how to proceed. One weekend, a group of us were out on Folly Beach and I was surfing, which I guess can be a bit of an aphrodisiac. (Actually, it definitely is—just google "surfer's wives.") I headed back to the beach and asked if Molly wanted to learn. Next thing I knew we were frolicking in the waves and laughing. This didn't seem like a bad precursor to a clandestine courtship. After our surf session, a week passed. I was out surfing again, trying to show off to no one in particular, and I did a backflip off my board, landing on my head on a rock jetty. I started to see stars and bleed, so I limped in and got a ride to the hospital, receiving seven stitches in my head.

I immediately called Molly and told her about the accident, making sure to embellish my athleticism and bravery. Then I politely asked if she'd pick me up from the hospital when I got my stitches out in a week's time. And she agreed!

So the following week I get to the hospital and tell the nurses that there is a girl I really like who is picking me up, and that I wanted to make her laugh. The nurses got excited and asked what I needed to accomplish my goal. I told them that my head had to be mummified, as in, the whole thing wrapped in gauze except for two eyeholes. I also needed a neck brace, and I needed the nurses to roll me out in a wheelchair, for good measure. They were amazingly cool and obliged me, rolling me out to see Molly when the time came. After I mumbled her name as if I had head trauma, to her horror, I ripped off the gauze, jumped out of the chair, and carried her in my arms to a beautiful surf and turf dinner with fine red wine. Okay, I'm making up the last part, but we did end up falling in love and dating for a year and half. And to think—I owe it all to a head wound!

While all my head injuries were pretty much self-inflicted, I can't exactly say the same about my dental problems. You see, that's mostly genetics. In case you need further proof that my mom is a saint, the bum dental genetics are all my dad's fault. The best dental days of my life were when I was five years old. Oh boy, I was peaking physically and dentally then. I was well proportioned, my arms weren't freakishly long, I had a little meat on my bones, I had a nice SMILE. Then my baby teeth fell out and it's been a struggle ever since. One of my teeth just never bothered to grow back. I mean, WTF? And another was like a little peg tooth. Like a pirate's leg next to a bunch of non-pirate normal legs. At one point I had a retainer with teeth attached to them, which provided plenty of laughs for the kids at school and which also partly explains my status as a late bloomer.

However, as girls started to become more important, my laid-back, self-deprecating attitude about my pearly whites started to change. I wanted studly and fully formed teeth, not peg-leg teeth. After having some minor dental work done and some new teeth inserted to improve my mouth, I eventually headed to college. My teeth were passable, until one bright sunny afternoon at Sanford Stadium as the Georgia Bulldogs took on the hated Tennessee Volunteers. I had a bunch of friends in town for the game, and wouldn't you know it, the Dawgs prevailed! After the game, we walked to a house party and I tackled my friend Robbie into some bushes. Standard postgame celebratory move. Robbie retaliated, dove down, and hit my ankle with his hand. My face hit the cement, hard, and there went my two fake teeth and most of the real ones, as well. Even I cringe at this.

Luckily my dentist in college ended up being a cool guy. He went to Phish concerts, so we swapped some fun stories. He definitely wasn't afraid of a good time. I thought I'd tasted the same nitrous from his office in a parking lot at the Fox Theatre in Atlanta. Just kidding. Somehow all of my dentists have been super cool people. I might actually harbor some regret that I didn't go down the dental path myself. I, too, could be a cool dentist. It's a very respectable profession, it's flexible, and it's typically not life-or-death. It would have saved me a lot of money, that's for sure. But I guess you have to study a decent amount in college to get into dental school, which would have been a challenge for me. Oh well.

Perhaps my fondest dental misadventure happened in Sonoma

County over the Fourth of July in 2009, when I was twenty-nine years old. This was the summer that a handful of my friends decided to meet in Seattle, party a little there, go up to the San Juan Islands and kayak with killer whales, then head down to the Yakima River to camp out for a night. After that, many of the guys went their separate ways. But me and my friend Kirk decided to keep the adventure going (this happens often in Shepland). We rented a car and drove down the Washington and Oregon coast, ending up in San Francisco, where we had a few friends.

Those San Francisco friends decided to plan a little trip to wine country for the holiday. Wine country was all new to us, so of course we were excited. Kirk's wife was flying out, and a celebration was to be had. The place our friends found was a ten-thousand-acre vineyard/ranch in the remote winding hills of Sonoma. The closest gas station was thirty minutes away. In addition to our clothes and shoes, we brought along a few pounds of mushrooms with us, and I don't mean portobello and shiitake.

We would eat mushrooms mixed in with breakfast, lunch, and dinner. Remember, kids, veggies are healthy! I knew about six of the thirty-five people who were there, but, as you might imagine if you've dined on this particular fungi, we all became fast friends. I was heavy into Toto at the time, mainly because of their song "Rosanna." It is a banger. I first got turned onto it because a friend sent me the music video, and I swear it's one of the funniest and strangest 1980s videos you'll ever see. It's a smorgasbord of mullets. The song is perfect for a post-lunch/pre-dinner mushroom dance session.

So that night, fueled by fungi, we decided to create a fake prom and get dressed up. We drew a member of the opposite sex's name out of a hat, and that was your date. We started having fun and dancing, and I put on Toto's "Rosanna" and the place went wild—all five of us. The other folks were riding bikes down a hill outside. Anyway, a handful of us were jumping around to "Rosanna" and then . . . it happened. Again.

A wayward knuckle belonging to my friend Bart made square contact with one of my fake teeth, and it flew across the dance floor as the warped slow-motion sound effect of me yelling "NOOOOOOO" rose above the music. My first thought was . . . *Okay, I'm tripping, and I can take this one of two ways. I can be stressed and panic, or I can celebrate the lost tooth!* After several seconds of internal mushroom dialogue/analysis, I decided to go with the latter and celebrate. After all, I had a prom to enjoy!

As fate would have it, my prom date's outfit was barefoot and pregnant. She had on a tight dress with a balloon in her stomach, and no shoes. I was toothless and wearing a beret! We were a perfect match. So again, what some might deem a tragedy was exactly what the Party Gods intended, and over my many years I have learned that you must trust these gods to achieve maximum bliss!

When the fun was over, I had to fly from San Francisco to Hilton Head Island without a tooth. And somehow I got upgraded to first class! We've all walked through an airplane past the first-class passengers, stealing glances at them to see who they are. I milked this short stroll through first class for all it was worth, smiling widely with my gap-toothed mouth at everyone I passed, basically proving that the "class" in first class was optional.

Writing about my personal injury adventures has caused me to become introspective, even as I cringe through the memories. Thinking back on all of my mishaps has made me think of a clichéd inspirational quote. I usually mock these types of quotes, so forgive me for this: "What doesn't kill you makes you stronger." Actually, I want to modify that saying—because it often hasn't made me stronger. I tore my MCL in season six of *Southern Charm* by riding a mechanical bull at a bar, an experience that didn't make me stronger physically or emotionally in any way whatsoever. I also separated my shoulder tackling a trash can in Dubai on the Fourth of July. That sucked. But guess what all these incidents did for me. They gave the fine people who will one day write my obituary or give my eulogy more than enough material to play with. It's a virtual treasure trove! So, you're welcome, friends and family!

I'll try to delay that inevitable fate for as long as I can by toning it down just a little. Not totally, but a little. My new saying is: "What doesn't kill you makes for a great story."

And now, I'm going to share some of my best advice about accidents and injuries, just in case you see me as an authority on the subject.

Personal- Injury Advice

1. Beware of heroics around a pool and/or cliff.

2. The best form of humor is wit. Yes, the prom queen might be drawn to the daredevil guy with the skateboard or the BMX bike, but eventually they'll just want someone who makes them laugh by mummifying their skull as a prank.

3. I'm not here to say don't climb trees, water-ski in an alligator-infested lagoon, or skydive (tandem with an expert). These are all risky activities that help you learn about yourself. So, go ahead.

4. The outdoors is a magical and sometimes dangerous place. Get out there and have fun. Break a bone or two. (But don't sue me if you do.)

5. Cause mischief but be contrite afterward. The "boys will be boys" defense is always there like a shining beacon until you're about fifteen or so.

6. Take calculated risks, but keep in mind that your demise will break your poor mother's heart. And we can't have that. But if she's not disappointed or slightly terrified by your actions, you haven't done the whole growing-up thing right. Sorry, Mom.

7. Getting your cast signed as a teen is tantamount to being a rock star on tour, with beautiful girls swarming around you, begging to make their mark. What I'm saying is, take injuries in stride, because you might just get some sympathy from a girl, which has usually worked out pretty well for me over the years. No shame in sympathy lovin'.

· CHAPTER 5 ·

THE ASSHOLE EQUATION

There's a quote from Bill Murray in the great book *Live From New York: The Complete, Uncensored History of* Saturday Night Live *as Told by Its Stars, Writers, and Guests*—a book that I devoured when it was published. After all, these were many of my heroes recounting their time on a show that broke ground, a show that I worshipped. One of my favorites (and let's face it, one of everyone's favorites) is Bill Murray, who just so happens to live in Charleston and who is part owner of our Minor League Baseball team, the RiverDogs.

People always ask if I've met Bill Murray because of the Charleston connection, and the answer is, yeah, I have! A few times. The first was at a party in Charleston for the finale of Danny McBride's hilarious HBO show *Vice Principals*, and Bill (if I can call him

"Bill") was there. I actually walked up to him and talked to him about golf and life in Charleston, and he was very pleasant, but then I screwed up and asked him for a picture, which he politely declined (he's known to be pretty private). He was nice as can be, but I felt like an asshole, and I deserved it. McBride—who I had met a few times before and who told me that he and his wife are big Bravo watchers and fans of *Southern Charm*—made fun of me. He basically laughed and told me he could have predicted that Murray would say no. It was a disaster, or at least it felt like it at the time. But it's good to be knocked down a peg every now and then. I've also seen Bill at bars in Charleston, and he usually gets mobbed and has to slip out the back. Another time, I was at a restaurant having a burger for lunch and Bill was there eating in a booth, and some random dude at the bar asked me if that was Bill Murray, so I said yes. Then the dude just slipped into the booth with Bill and asked him for a photo, which made me cringe for many reasons, but mostly because I have actually been THAT GUY. In any case, now I always try to give Bill (or Mr. Murray?) space.

After so many seasons of *Southern Charm* I have a little perspective on what it's like to be in a public place and have people know who you are. And honestly, for me, it's been an overwhelmingly positive experience. People just want a quick picture or they want to buy you a shot or a drink. I chat for a moment and that's it. It can actually be quite lovely. And it's really easy to be nice. It's hard to be a jerk. To be dismissive of people who just want to say hello is just bad karma in my book. Then again, we don't know what it's like for someone of Mr. Murray's stature. I surmise it's a whole different ball game. Everyone feels connected to you. And I mean everyone—these guys just have generations of fans. It's insane.

I've gotten to hang out with a few *Saturday Night Live* cast members over the past few years, and they are the sharpest, wittiest people—I spent most of the time just trying to mentally keep up with them. Every minute there was a new ridiculous joke being offered up. I loved it. Anyway, I was talking to Will Forte once and I asked him whether it was hard for him to deal with fame and being in public, because I was a little curious (this was after *Southern Charm*'s third season, so people were starting to recognize me—not that I'm comparing myself to an *SNL* comedian, but I wanted to know). And Will said something like, "Man, for me it's not bad at all. You should see what it's like going somewhere with Will Ferrell!" This is all a very long and winding path back to a Bill Murray quote from that *SNL* book that I love. He said, "When you become famous, you've got like a year or two where you act like a real asshole. You can't help yourself. It happens to everybody. You've got like two years to pull it together—or it's permanent."

Despite what you might think of me from the show or from the people who scream at me via social media, I think of that quote a lot.

I fully admit that there are certain instances on *Southern Charm* over the past seven years that one could point to and say, "But, Shep, you were a dick right there. And there. Oh, and there too." And you'd have a good case. I do hope that if you've watched every season, you've seen some glimpses of humanity and shreds of kindness in me over the years. Hopefully you'd see me as someone who likes to have fun and rib friends along the way. What you won't see is that I'm friends with every single cast member behind the scenes. Some more than others, but there is no lingering animosity on my side toward anyone. I've said some hurtful things on camera, and off. Nothing that is irreparable, though, and my close friends on and off the show know my true character, which is basically that of one happy guy. How could I not be, honestly? Remember Shepland?

Sometimes, though, the pot must be stirred, and sometimes it's a hell of a lot of fun to stir it. For example, when we went to Hilton Head in season five and Thomas and Ashley were acting crazy, I walked up to Naomie and Cameran and blurted, "I fucking hate her!" Or all the times I get bored at a party and pick a fight with Craig for no reason, just to add some drama.

The show has given me lots of laughs and plenty of opportunities. And just like any endeavor that we care about in life that we want to see do well, you BETTER be passionate about it. The problem is, there are a lot of cooks in the kitchen, and there's no way you're all going to like the soufflé that comes out of the oven every episode and every season. But I'd be crazy to tell you I wish I'd never done *Southern Charm*. I tell people it's a 75 percent satisfying and fun ride. That's a pretty damn good hit rate in life. And to all the cast members, producers, and executives out there who I've worked with over the years, if I've been cutting, sarcastic, or mean-spirited, I'm truly sorry. It's because I care. Seriously I do. I want the show to be as authentic, funny, and amazing as possible. And it has been all those things way more than it hasn't. There's been too much love and laughter to look at it any other way.

So although I'm nowhere near the stature of Mr. Murray and his castmates on the first few years of *SNL* from a notoriety standpoint, after a few years of "fame," I'm confident that I haven't changed all that much since . . . well, let's see. Maybe college? If someone truly thinks I'm an asshole, they certainly haven't spent any time with me, and their complaints are just noise from the cheap seats. I admit I haven't really evolved all that much, which may be problematic. But I certainly haven't been on a high horse with people I encounter from day to day. I like interacting with folks. I'm a gregarious and collegial guy. I've got a great family and group of friends and I live near the beach in a house of my own. It's like a dream.

I have commented many times that I don't suffer fools gladly, and I stand by that. But I love foolishness. I also like to be around thoughtful and engaging people—people who have knowledge of a subject that maybe I don't, or people who are passionate about something, anything. Though I fully admit that sometimes I can be a pseudo-intellectual, at least I can admit it and at least I'm trying! I love watching documentaries and reading nonfiction. I want to learn as much as I can. But the most important characteristic one can have is a sense of humor about themselves. And usually people who don't are idiots. And I don't suffer them gladly. And I never will. But I'll also try to follow Mr. Murray's advice and not act like an asshole about it.

If we're being very honest, being drunk on TV (or being drunk anytime, really) can turn even the most mild-mannered chap into a raging asshole from time to time. I would actually categorize myself as a happy drunk, and I take pride in that, like some people take pride in the fact that they're a Nobel laureate or a neurosurgeon. Some people are *not* happy drunks. Some of my close friends and family are emotional when they drink. The worst kind. Jerry Seinfeld said it best when he said, "I hate being around alcoholics because they're either telling you how much they love you or how much they hate you." That's my nightmare. Being a happy drunk, on the other hand, means you can almost get away with anything. I mean, I've never had my ass kicked (outside of a heated Nintendo game in the early nineties), and that says a lot. I've been running my mouth for a long time, but I always find a way to turn it into a funny situation and lighten the moment with some laughter. I always stay away from the dark side, like a devoted Jedi.

That said, I have had some asshole moments. Big ones.

After *Southern Charm* season six I was pretty disillusioned. And to be honest, I can be elitist as fuck, but it's not my default setting, and it's not something I'm proud of. But I can get nasty if a certain mood hits. During that time, I had an incident on Instagram where I was walking down the street in New York with friends, laughing and jeering at everything I saw and posting it for all the world to see. It rightfully appeared as if I was making fun of a homeless person who had collected a pile of cans. In the video, I said, "Nice cans," which is a line from the movie *European Vacation* and which is a dumb reference that's only funny if you're hammered and with idiotic friends trying to one-up each other. In reality it was a (just as unfunny and insensitive) joke about boobs. Once I sobered up, I regretted it. I was pissed at myself for even getting into a frame of mind where I wouldn't care who was hurt, all because I wanted to get a laugh. That's not who I am. I'm not the schoolyard bully, but I was so smashed and my lack of awareness that night is astonishing to me.

I had a rough season and off-season in 2019. I'd love to sit down for supper with anyone who judged me negatively and decided I was a jerk during that time and calmly explain what transpired from my point of view, but that's not how this world works, does it? Anyhow, I was feeling extremely down. The worst part was that I felt like much of it was by my own sword, which made me feel doubly bad because I always thought of myself as a somewhat clever person who doled out advice, rather than someone who was unhappy and desperately seeking it.

After all of this, I started talking to a shrink at the insistence of a good friend. Friends were worried about me. Hell, *I* was worried about me. The shrink and I talked on the phone for an hour as I sat in a Harris Teeter grocery store parking lot. We talked about life. We talked about drugs and alcohol, which I know I've touted a bit here in the pages of this book. I certainly have had more than a few instances where drugs and alcohol have been my worst enemy and given me a false sense of being bulletproof, and made me think I was brilliant when I was actually being boorish.

We also talked about other things I was passionate about, and the fact that for some, boredom can lead to poor decision-making—especially when you're on a show that films four months a year and then you have a ton of free time. It's a potentially dangerous situation because you feel like, "Hey, I made another season, who cares what happens next!" Idle hands are a devil's workshop, as they say. I started to tell the shrink about a few things I was thinking about and working on, and he remarked how my whole persona changed when I talked about those projects, and he suggested that I focus on those things. He also wanted to know whether I even cared about negative press, which I found interesting. Because I guess the old dictum of "any press is good press" gets in people's minds as a defense mechanism. I think he sensed that I didn't relish bad press, and he was right. Again, I go back to my childhood days, when I learned that being rambunctious was okay but being a "bad egg" was not. The thought of bringing embarrassment to family and friends is just devastating and appalling to me. That's not to say it hasn't happened.

I thought the conversation with the shrink was constructive, but I was also a bit embarrassed about the stigma that therapy brings with it in some people's minds. I'm reminded of a scene in *Crocodile Dundee* where Sue tells Mick about a woman in New York City who benefited from psychiatry. And he said something like "Doesn't she have any mates?" That's how I saw it for a long time—if you have a bunch of good friends and a loving family, why would you need to talk to a third party? Then I heard a Conan O'Brien podcast with Howard Stern, and they both were very open and honest about how much therapy had helped them in their lives. And those are two of my heroes! So that gave me pause. It occurred to me that BECAUSE a therapist is a third party is the exact reason that they are valuable! They don't have a dog in the fight. They're completely objective. And they are trained professionals with tools that can help you in certain situations. With your family and friends, they know you and you know them. If they mention something critical, you could get defensive and say, "Well, what about you!" It's imperative to just have a sounding board, I think, especially during tough times.

I ended up finding an ongoing therapist in Charleston, and she's been a big help. Without going into too much detail, her advice can best be condensed into the old Johnny Mercer song "Accentuate the Positive." Be more strategic, without being conniving. Sometimes retreat a little to advance later. Jesus, it sounds like I'm describing Sun Tzu's military tome, *The Art of War*, but the therapist listened to me, and I think gathered that I was engaging and happy, but that I had produced lots of anxieties due to stupid (often show-related) quarrels, and a lot of it was because of my impulsiveness and passion. With success comes frustration and head butting/horn locking with others. I was also acting spoiled because things have gone my way a lot in life. Looking back, I even see getting kicked out of school as a positive. But then again, rationalizing poor behavior and missteps by saying, "It's part of my journey, bro," is irresponsible and fake spiritual.

Now the stakes are much higher, and so my awareness must grow with that. I have to rise above pettiness. I love the saying "Don't wrestle with a pig. You just get dirty and the pig enjoys it." That was my interpretation of her advice. I sound like a bad self-help guru. The trick is to come out looking like Wilbur from

Charlotte's Web—totally innocent and spared from the slaughter-house. Anyway, the therapist and I talked about season seven of *Southern Charm*, and I expressed trepidation about wanting to do it again, since I felt like I didn't come out of the sixth season looking my best. Each season I have to take stock of how things went. Sometimes you come out looking like the villain, and sometimes you're the court jester, which is my favorite. But that season I felt like a villain. I try not to listen to the hate on social media, but I wouldn't be human if it didn't wear me down at times. So I always have to gauge whether it's worth doing the next season. The therapist made me do a pros and cons list and, wouldn't you know it, the pros won. I'm not sure if that'll always be the case, but for now that's the score.

We also talk about my attitudes and decisions in my romantic life, and I discovered that I always get pessimistic and assume relationships will end (despite the fact that my parents have a long and happy marriage). I get anxiety about relationships ending or hearts getting broken, and she said something that really opened my eyes. She said, "Do you think you're the only one who has anxiety about relationships? Who doesn't wonder what might happen if they meet someone else? This is universal and it's a fact of life. Life is unpredictable, especially when you add another person."

Of course, she's 100 percent right. It's a philosophical theory many have expressed, but I like this description from the writer Claudia Gray the best:

We are all the center of our own universe, and all of us in someone else's orbit. It's a paradox, but sometimes paradoxes are where the truth begins.

If I didn't mention before, I'm a huge fan of the truth. So despite what it might look like on the show or on social media from time to time, I think about being fair and decent to everyone I come across. Sometimes I succeed, sometimes not. Sometimes not being an asshole takes work! Maybe Mr. Murray was just partly right with his equation. Maybe it takes a little longer than two years to figure out how NOT to be an asshole. Maybe it takes six and a half years? Maybe it takes really examining yourself and trying to achieve some sort of Zen about this strange world that you inhabit, whether that world is played out on TV or not. Maybe, to riff on Alexander Pope, to be an asshole is human, to figure out how *not* to be an asshole is divine.

When Bill Murray and his castmates started up at *SNL*, there wasn't Twitter, Instagram, or *US Weekly* (although there have always been tabloids). I'd love to see some footage of their insane parties with Keith Richards, David Bowie, and Robin Williams—I'm sure it was totally low-key and no one acted like an asshole *ever*. The terrain is just a lot rockier and fraught with peril these days, with potential land mines (aka social media) everywhere. Honestly, I would be suspicious of anyone who has been in the public eye for any amount of time who HASN'T faced some sort of embarrassing moment or minor scandal. Even a saint like Tom Hanks was embroiled in a minor semi-scandal when he was quarantined with coronavirus in Australia and he shared a video of himself eating Vegemite on toast, causing Aussies to BLOW UP at him because he didn't have the correct Vegemite-to-bread ratio on his toast. *Everyone* has demons and skeletons. The more you try to suppress and hide them, the stronger they become and the more the soup comes to a violent boil. You have to acknowledge and understand those demons so you can see them looming on the horizon. I'm not saying I'm an expert at this, but I am trying. And it has been more than two years since I've been in the public eye, so to speak, so according to Bill Murray's asshole equation, my time for being a true asshole is up.

In honor of the Asshole Equation, I present to you my official list of the best/worst assholes in film/TV history, so you can learn from their mistakes (and also go back and watch some great shows).

1. **Johnny from *Karate Kid*:** The actor is named William Zabka (his friends supposedly call him Billy), and my friends and I are obsessed with him. The guy was also in *National Lampoon's European Vacation*, where he bangs Audrey's best friend and utters the famous phrase "I miss the shit out of you!" Anyway, in *Karate Kid* he's the rich asshole who is just a major bully toward Daniel LaRusso (the new guy, the little guy, the freaking KARATE KID). A few things in defense of Johnny: LaRusso was chasing after his ex-girlfriend, so that was cause for tension. Also, if you look closely during the bathroom scene, Johnny is actually sitting on the toilet rolling a joint (I missed that detail for many years) and Daniel douses him with water, ruining the weed (not cool). At the very end, Johnny actually insists on giving Daniel the trophy. So, like many of us, he may be a redeemable asshole? The real villain

in the movie is actually Cobra Kai dojo sensei John Kreese, who created the atmosphere of bullying and general asshole-ness that Johnny was reared in. The actor's name is Martin Kove, and I'm also obsessed with him, to the point where, during college, I made a website in his honor. The website was devoted to finding Martin Kove more work, and we had no clue what we were doing, so it was really just a bunch of photos of him in *Karate Kid* and *Commando*. It's a safe bet that our rudimentary online résumé didn't land the guy any roles. Anyway, in *Karate Kid* he was teaching all those kids to be little pricks and show no mercy. They were so impressionable, and it's all his fault. They had to unlearn how to be assholes. Fuck him! The lesson here is: Behind every asshole, there might be an even bigger asshole.

2. **King Edward Longshanks from *Braveheart*:** This guy insists that all the English lords in Scotland have sex with newly married brides! He also fires arrows into his own troops. AND he kills his son's boyfriend. Anti-gay medieval kings can go fuck themselves. But what a brilliant piece of acting. Lesson: Don't discriminate, and don't shoot arrows at your friends. It's rude.

3. **King Joffrey and Ramsay from *Game of Thrones*:** This one is a tie. Although I wanted to absolutely beat the shit out of Joffrey every time he was on-screen, I was legit scared of Ramsay. Apparently, I wasn't the only one. Supposedly the guy who played Joffrey took a break from acting and literally had to hide from the public because people thought he was that asshole character. That sucks,

because that's really a testament to how well he crushed the role. Lesson: Being an asshole can ruin your career.

4. **Walter Peck in** *Ghostbusters*: In honor of Bill Murray, this is the *Ghostbusters* villain who releases all the ghosts into New York City. The actor also plays the opportunistic/idiot/sabotaging reporter in *Die Hard* and *Die Hard 2*. I'm noticing a trend here. All these guys are pretty good actors, judging by the fact that years later I still spend a lot of time thinking about how much of a dick they are/ were. Lesson: Don't be a dick, and don't unleash any ghosts.

5. **Sawyer from** *Lost*: God, I hated this guy! I despised him for many reasons, the biggest one being that he is able to seduce Kate (Evangeline Lilly), who I was extremely smitten with and who I wanted Jack to end up with. The hot-dude villain is a fun role to play, I bet. I actually met Josh Holloway (who played Sawyer) at an NBC event. I must admit, despite my hatred of his character, I was like a little fangirl. His charisma just drew me in. So, I get it, Kate. You are forgiven. Lesson: Assholes can be charismatic as fuck.

Southern Charm Bios

When *Southern Charm* began, we were each asked to write a short bio for the Bravo.com website. I think I rightly assumed that not many viewers were curious enough to go to the website and dig deeper about a bunch of strangers in Charleston, and after watching a few early episodes, many of you were probably scared about what you'd find out. I took the bio as a challenge to be as silly and outrageous as I possibly could and to show off some writing chops (and remember, I didn't even know if the show would last past one season, so what did I have to lose?). The bio gave my friends in the Bravo offices some joy, and they claimed to like it. I'm not sure how many fans comb Bravo.com for *Southern Charm* bios, though, so here they are for a (hopefully) wider audience. These bios also gave me the chance to write about myself in the third person, which is a wildly absurd thing to do. Think of them as my early flirtation with literary greatness!

SEASON 1

This one was just a Q&A. When they asked me to list my occupation, I wrote: raconteur.

SEASON 2

Over a year has passed since we've last seen Mr. Shepard "Shep" Rose navigating the sometimes turbulent waters of the great city of

Charleston. While he hasn't changed, he has definitely evolved. Shep is still his roguish and irreverent self; however, time has softened some rough edges and allowed him to cultivate a number of endeavors. He's opened up a new restaurant and bar called the Palace Hotel that served gourmet hot dogs, tacos, and cold beverages in an "off the beaten path" neighborhood in downtown Charleston. He also built a home in the same neighborhood, and has begun renovations on an old nightclub nearby that should be ready this spring. He's finally, after thirty-five years on this earth, starting to understand the basic tenets of adulthood. These may be the self-proclaimed halcyon days for Mr. Rose. However, he's also aware of the old dictum "Just when you think you have it all figured out, the rug is pulled out from under you." So Shep intends to remain vigilant, expose fraud, and fight injustice. In short, he will not rest on his laurels.

SEASON 3

Almost three years have passed since we first met Mr. Rose. Many questions have been answered and curiosities satiated. However, do we really know the real Shep? Does anyone? Is he a fast-talking charlatan with the depth of a rain puddle? Or an intelligent, thoughtful, and supportive denizen of the booming metropolis of Charleston? Does he even know the answer to these questions?

What we do know is that the Ship (Shep) is on course and maintaining current cruising speed. Wind in its sails, booty secured in the galley. No doldrums on the horizon for this journey. Traveling remains a passion, as does socializing. One may ask if this sort of peripatetic life wears thin on a man. Shep would answer emphatically NO. It never does, and hopefully never will. For a rolling stone gathers no moss.

SEASON 4

For this bio the higher-ups at Bravo asked me if I had any changes to my last bio, and my reply was: "You're goddamn right I have some changes. This is my favorite assignment of the year."

As we approach season four, it should be noted that there are four seasons in a calendar year. Thus, if analyzed cyclically, Mr. Shepard Rose has indeed come full circle. Ergo, season one began in the summer. So, we now find him in the spring of his television existence. Indeed, Mr. Rose is in full bloom! As the old saying goes, "The whole is greater than the sum of its parts." Shep happily plays the part of court jester in this amalgam/ensemble of colorful characters that is *Southern Charm.* However, this season Shep grapples with the Falstaffian allusion that the joviality of a clown often masks a certain sadness and avoidance of responsibility and/or accountability. However, his acknowledgment of this looming identity shows a self-awareness that may allow him to get ahead of the curve and make the necessary adjustments in order to avoid clichéd pitfalls and double binds.

This season, without revealing too much, we see Shep living

downtown in the house he built last year, enjoying all the tomfoolery that bar ownership affords and seems to invite. Indeed, good times are had. Women, wine, and song will get you every time, though, and Shep is wondering if the late nights and mornings are taking their toll. Is the love of a good and honest woman the answer and salve that can bring him back from the fringe? Perhaps, but he will not compromise and settle for anything less than true love. For why settle down when you can settle up (at the bar)?

SEASON 5

Believe it or not, we are entering the fifth season of *Southern Charm*. It's similar to the fifth dimension, which was an attempt to develop a theory that unifies the four fundamental forces in nature: strong and weak nuclear forces, gravity, and electromagnetism. For *Southern Charm* has largely propagated the properties of physics: inertia, pressure, gravity, the bending of time. We have seen this cast of characters develop in front of our very eyes! Like a gentle tide, many have surged and receded to the delight and/or dismay of those around them and the viewers at home alike. And now, as Shakespeare so eloquently wrote about war: "Once more unto the breach, dear friends, once more." (Not that this is the final season, although it could be; alas, Mr. Rose is just a player upon a stage.)

This year has Mr. Shepard Rose in a state of sedation. He put his heart out into the harsh and unforgiving climate of deep romance and it tragically yielded to the elements. So now he sits in his lonely castle of solitude on the shores of the Atlantic plotting his return and regaining his strength. Through it all Mr. Rose is surprisingly pleased with how life has brought him to this nexus. He's coming to grips with the fact that he's no longer a young man, but he also realizes that he'll never lose that adolescent spark and roguish spirit. So now he must find a balance. And he believes that this current lifestyle is the beginning of a new and exciting chapter. He has scars and he won't hide them. At the risk of sounding trite, he will "pick his spots" and "keep things simple," all while continuing to strive for happiness and extemporaneous adventure.

SEASON 6

Relationshep was a nickname bestowed upon Mr. Shepard Rose in the year A.D. 2003. Although not fully domesticated, could Mr. Rose for once care about someone other than himself? One would think his closest comrades would evoke happiness and admiration for his newfound condition; however, their forked tongue revealed itself as they lamented the absence of the affable idiot they once knew. But alas, nothing lasts forever, and Shep Rose (like a phoenix from the ashes) returned to his friends' hilarious and sophomoric bosom, where the tomfoolery, debauchery, and patently asinine comradery persisted for many years.

Many years have passed and good times had. We now find Mr. Rose's cohorts married with families. No longer does laughter bellow down the hallways of the dormitory of life. The same jokes fall on different ears, it's all been done before; the once spontaneous has become mundane. Mr. Rose is starting to feel as if his old moniker (Relationshep) beckons him to return to a simpler time, where love reigned supreme. He fondly remembers grocery shopping, good-naturedly ruining a lovely girl's attempts at preparing an edible meal, reluctantly agreeing to watch a stupid TV show that she likes, then secretly becoming obsessed with it.

But where to look? Has he been riding on the prairie for too long? Scanning the horizon for greener pastures in lieu of building on a plot of land that was fertile, defensible, and provided comfort and calmness? Has life passed Shep by? He'd answer: Of course not! For the average life expectancy for an American male is 78.74 years. Mr. Rose is almost on the back nine of life. He seeks change; he wishes to perhaps evolve and show to himself and those around him that he is capable of maturation. He loves Charleston, but has all the good land been tilled? Perhaps it has, so he intends to heed Horace Greeley's famous proclamation and supplication, "Go West, young man!" Manifest destiny just might be the answer for Mr. Rose, for he will seek his better half on the roads leading out of his home state and pray that it does not become a trail of tears!

SEASON 7

Redemption is a word, nay a concept, that has been around since the dinosaurs. It means our sins are washed away. Down into the drain, trickling to the nearest river and eventually finding their way to the Cape of Good Hope. The result is a naked person. Clean and reborn. Nervous but sanguine.

This is where we find Mr. Shep Rose at the dawn of season seven. He has suffered the slings and arrows of outrageous fortune. Mostly self-inflicted wounds, which sting the most. But here he is: wiser, humbled, determined to right the wrongs and evolve into a man in full. Although we've heard this rhetoric in the past, Shep realizes that sometimes you must lose it all to really gain enlightenment. At least he thinks he remembers reading that in the book *Siddhartha*.

Lil Craig (the dog) has been a shining beacon of happiness and joy. Not only to Shep, but to the whole fair city of Charleston. For how can life be burdensome when that little furry stalwart is waiting in the wings, wanting to play and eat treats?

In a twist almost no one saw coming, least of all Mr. Rose, there has been a new member of the team added last winter. For he has found a young woman who has made his little heart sing. Without revealing too much: She is kind, beautiful, and has a boatload of patience and understanding. The latter being very important.

Shep will enter this season contrite, centered, happy, and more than willing to mend any fence and even create newer and stronger alliances. He is not naked and afraid. He's naked and dating. Oh, and redeemed (depending on who you talk to.)

CHAPTER 6

OLIVER TRYST

There are two types of men in this world: You're either a Jeff Bridges or a Leonardo DiCaprio.

Not to say that either path is right or wrong, but the contrast is stark.

I'll start with Jeff. He's the son of actor Lloyd Bridges, who was a serious actor until he appeared in the Airplane franchise and *Hot Shots*, where he displayed amazing straight-man-plays-a-fool comedic acting chops. He and Leslie Nielsen are two of my favorites. Their slapstick skills are Oscar-worthy, and I could talk about their comedy skills for hours, but I'll spare you my armchair movie commentary.

Let's get back to Jeff.

As the son of a famous actor and a really handsome dude (google his early work; chicks dug him), Jeff Bridges probably could have cut a wide swath through Hollywood and had flings with any babe he wanted. And honestly, I don't know what he did until 1975 (when he was twenty-six!), when he met a gal who was waitressing in Montana, where he was shooting a film. He married her and had three daughters, and by all accounts he is the most normal family man you'd ever want to meet. This is actually confirmed by some of my San Francisco friends (the ones I had such a good time with when I was toothless in Sonoma). One of their buddies married one of Jeff's daughters, and they went to the wedding. Besides Jackson Browne playing at the reception, they said it was completely down-to-earth and everyone was cool, including Jeff.

My point about him is that he chose to walk a path that many others do, which on its surface doesn't seem earth-shattering. I mean, people stay married all the time. Actually, more like 50 percent of the time. But to do it while being wildly successful in an industry surrounded by beautiful people just begging to sleep with you does deserve a tip of the cap. I mean, temptation is a motherfucker. Imagine having T-bone steaks dangled in front of you at all times but you continue to eat chicken. Why would you do that if you love steak . . . and lobster, and potatoes au gratin, and salmon, and braised lamb. Dammit, now I'm hungry. I do hate to objectify women by comparing them to food, but I'm fine with women saying that guys are a hunk (of what, I'm not sure—hamburger meat?). What about calling a guy a beefcake? Not that anyone under sixty years old uses that term anymore, but still. My point is, I am not trying to objectify women, and if a woman made an analogy about me, I would hope it would have to do with a sirloin or beef Wellington (I like the pastry crust). Maybe I'm fighting a losing battle here, though, so let's move on.

I have a theory that might help explain the Jeff Bridges type of guy. Many all-time great athletes are married and start a family young and they go on to excel at a very high level. I wonder if there's a correlation? Once you take chasing girls and carrying on with your friends out of the equation, you probably fall into the old routine and gravitate toward practicing your craft, if for no other reason than to get the hell out of the house! Tennis greats Roger Federer, Rafael Nadal, and Novak Djokovic have all been with the same woman virtually their whole career, and that stability and routine might play a part in their success. I'm not a scientist or psychologist, but I believe my theory is 100 percent true.

Look at other athletic stalwarts. LeBron James, Michael Jordan, Steph Curry, Dwyane Wade, Peyton Manning, Joe Montana, and Jack Nicklaus all married their high school or college girlfriends, or got married early in their career. They might not still be with them now, and the marriages might not have been perfect, but they were married early. Now, the other guys who enjoyed the spoils of fame like free booze and plentiful women? I doubt they had the staying power that the aforementioned guys had. The prime example is NFL champ Joe Namath, a notorious drinker and lothario. Yes, he won one of the most famous Super Bowls of all time, but if you look at his career statistics, his numbers aren't that great (did you know he threw 173 touchdowns and had 220 interceptions!). His one outstanding season is why he's remembered with such admiration. That, and all the women he bedded. But my point is that he didn't have, say, TEN seasons of glory, possibly because he never settled down until he was forty-one years old, which is ancient in football years. Look at Tom Brady! Married. My point is that I have an unscientific theory linking athletic glory and marriage, and I'm sticking to it.

On the opposite end of the spectrum from the Jeff Bridgeses of the world, we have Leonardo DiCaprio. He gains stardom at an early age since he's a gifted actor. He forms a small group of friends, and they call themselves the "pussy posse," which is incredibly douchey, but so were they probably. Think about it: You're a drama major/actor as a kid and teen, so you definitely weren't "cool" as a theater kid, not like the quarterback of the football team. In fact, you probably got your ass kicked by the quarterback. These guys longingly stared at the prom queen, hoping and wishing that somehow, they would be attracted to them and their love of acting. No such luck, until the *Titanic* hits the iceberg and then . . . it's ON!

So post-*Titanic*, imagine that young Leo has got some catching up to do. Suddenly all the doors/women are unlocked. Who can blame you for walking (or sleeping) your way through them? You'd be crazy not to! And maybe my theory of success and marriage has just been blown to pieces by Leo DiCaprio, because he's in his forties and he's notorious for never settling down and only dating younger models, and he's crazy successful. (For the record, I thought his Oscar-winning movie *The Revenant* was good, not great, but it was so beautiful to look at, it inspired me to book a trip to Alaska.) Like I said, I am not a psychologist or a scientist.

I'm just a guy trying to solve the eternal riddle that is commitment.

Also, I know I boldly said there were two different types of men in the world, but actually there might be a third type: the George Clooney/Derek Jeter/Warren Beatty guy. The proud bachelor who eventually settles down. Yes, take away their many accomplishments and talents, and THESE GUYS ARE ME! All of them excelled in their professional and private lives. Which is to say, their incredibly enviable private exploits didn't seem to interfere with their careers. But that has nothing to do with me (I don't really have or want a career). It's their approach and philosophy of life and love that maybe I've subconsciously adopted. From where I sit, it looks to me like these guys realized that life is short . . . check that, they realized that life is LONG, and women are everywhere! I doubt any of these guys had any trouble with women at any point in their lives, but they saw no reason to rush into a legally binding contract with anyone or to have little kids running around taking away their freedom to live life to the fullest, and to travel and have guiltless spontaneous romances. To be footloose and fancy-free. A girl in every port. If it ain't broke, don't fix it. For a rolling stone gathers no moss. The road to excess leads to the palace of wisdom. Insert the lyrics to Lynyrd Skynyrd's "Free Bird"! You get what I mean.

These men sucked the marrow out of life and left no stone unturned. They gallivanted around the world and made memories that we mortal men could only dream about. They dated women who were on the cover of every magazine on earth (which has to be intoxicating) and they didn't apologize to anyone (hell, Beatty had a hit song written partially about him called "You're So Vain" by Carly Simon). But, here's the kicker—they all settled down eventually. They understood that perhaps life isn't truly enriching without a family.

I have another theory, because in Shepland, there is ample time to dream up theories: I think we were put on this earth for a very short time and we were meant to have fun. But it's undeniable that we were also (at least originally) put here to propagate our species. Now, we could get into topics like overpopulation and ill-advised excessive procreation, but I'll spare you. But I believe people when they say that having a child is the best thing they've ever done with their lives. I've never had one, but I understand that logic. What could be cooler than creating a little facsimile of yourself, who you then have the chance to actually fine-tune to be an even better version? And then you get to watch them flourish and then fall and get back up—what an unmitigated thrill ride that must be. I also believe that if there is a God or higher power, he or she didn't want us to come here and chase our every desire and whim, and to live like early Roman emperors Caligula and Nero, who were disgusting in their excess (no palace of wisdom for you assholes!). I think that we are meant to learn sacrifice and restraint at some point in our lives. In essence, and to steal Tom Wolfe's novel's name, to become A Man in Full.

From where I sit, I predict that in fifty years, marriage as we know it will be unrecognizable. The institution won't go extinct, but it'll be endangered. Granted, there will always be traditionalists who harken back to the old days and yearn for simpler times. These are the people who also try to slow tourism in Charleston (too late for that) and bemoan the end of VHS tapes. Though I empathize and somewhat agree with them, the horses are out of the barn, the train has left the station. Charleston is repeatedly named one of the top cities in the country by Condé Nast (did we think no one was paying attention?), and the olden days are done. What will cohabitation and "marriage" look like in the future? I believe it will become more of a self-defined partnership. It'll be more pragmatic and less idealistic. Because let's face it, it's fucking hard to be in a relationship. Being single is easy as pie. Attaching yourself to another human being is hard work, which is why I have headed into my forties as an unmarried man, like Warren Beatty and George Clooney, without the Oscars.

Dating sites and the internet are no friends of traditional marriage, either. I mean, there are even dating sites for married people! There are sites for sugar daddies, geeks, people who love Star Trek, or farmers only. Maybe I should start a dating app for seniors called Carbon Dating. The point is, the ability to connect with anyone you want is just insane. The interconnectivity means you can be in Maine and find and interact with someone in Washington State who has the same little proclivities or idiosyncrasies that you do, or meet three people a week who have your exact same taste in music. With so many options, why would you settle? In the past, you met a local girl or guy and you liked them and you were compatible and you're getting to a certain age, and you just threw your hands up and pulled the trigger (I'm nothing if not romantic). Some couples claim that it was love at first sight (or site) and their relationship just blossomed ever since. I don't buy that. There is a great Chris Rock stand-up line that comes to mind: "Men do not settle down. Men surrender."

It's tongue-in-cheek but mostly true. I think Chris Rock did end up getting divorced, so surrender isn't always permanent. Guys love thinking they still "have it" after they commit, and fantasizing that they are semi-available, if the situation presents itself. That's wishful thinking. Of course, I can't speak for all women or even one woman, but I sense that they like getting dolled up from time to time so they can walk into a bar or restaurant and feel beautiful or desirable, even if they're in a relationship. I once believed that women were more loyal and less promiscuous than men, but Lord have mercy, Instagram has opened my eyes! Women are just as scandalous and amorous as men, and then some. I'm all for it.

I wish I knew that some women felt this way when I was a late bloomer coming into my own. I thought girls were like a safe you had to unlock (that's better than comparing them to food, right?), and that they were always on the defense. It was almost like boys had to be on their best behavior and wait patiently until a girl was ready to get physical. Boy, was I wrong. Or maybe I was right? Maybe this is just the result of a great liberation or a slow erosion of the stigma against promiscuity? Maybe it was *Sex and the City* that changed it all? Whatever it is that helped women become more in-your-face sexually, I fully support it! "Well-behaved women rarely make history," right? Dammit I'm speaking in platitudes again. But that's a good one.

Before you tear me to shreds about my observations, let me clarify. I realize that to many girls this notion of sleeping around or one-night stands seems incomprehensible. That's fine, because to each their own. But for me, when I hear of the high school sweethearts who get married young it makes me shake my head in disgust (just kidding, but it does make me skeptical). Yes, on one level it's admirable but also . . . having sex with ONE PERSON? Come on. Variety is the spice of life, and also different experiences make you value the person you end up with (I think). This isn't the 1950s, thank God. I am not judging anyone who wants to wait to settle down. How could I? Men or women. I am all for equal rights when it comes to sleeping around until the last possible moment, or until you finally meet your Annette or Amal.

I was talking to an acquaintance recently who has a daughter in her early teens, and I was inquiring about college and whether he's nervous for her to start that next phase, since as men we KNOW how some college guys think. His answer was "Man, of course I am, but I raised her well and obviously I don't want to know any details, but I trust her to gain experience and hopefully choose the right person and maybe choose the wrong one a couple times because that's all part of it." This made total sense to me. It's not like in today's world you can be the dad with a pitchfork or a shotgun waiting for your little girl to be dropped off at 11:00 p.m. sharp. That will definitely not fly with a teenage girl on Instagram. By the way, I reserve the right to change my tune if and when I have a daughter! I may suddenly start believing that no one should have sex until marriage, but time will tell.

On that note, here's another line from Chris Rock's stand-up that's a little more complicated: "Men are only as faithful as their options."

This one is a matter of faithfulness and character in many instances, but it's also real, due to a four-letter word spelled *L.U.S.T.* Lust is a powerful, undeniable force. It drives us to make some stupid decisions and also allows us to experience pure bliss at times. It should not and cannot be ignored. Again, unless I one day have a daughter, in which case she can ignore lust all she wants.

When it comes to options, there is also the matter of the one-night stand, which seems to mean different things to different people. I was with a group of people once and we were playing an infantile card game that doubled as a drinking game (I hated the game but I participated nonetheless). We were supposed to raise our hand if we'd ever had a one-night stand. One very cute girl did not raise her hand, but then she proceeded to sleep with a guy at the table that very night—and they haven't repeated the act since. A week later I was hanging out with one of her girlfriends and I said, "I guess she has to raise her hand now, since she had a one-night stand?" To my surprise, her girlfriend said her friend's post-card game tryst didn't qualify as a one-night stand since she knew the guy she slept with. For the record, they were not close at all, and had maybe met once before in passing. Call me insane, but to me that sounds like a one-night stand.

I'm not judging at all. In fact, I was happy for them both since I'm a firm believer in the ancient creed "If it feels good, do it." So

I'm not sure why some people still stigmatize something like a one-night stand. Look at women like Cardi B, Rihanna, and Samantha from *Sex and the City*, who put their sexuality out there with no reservations and with no shame, and look how many women love them. They own their sexuality. Most women have many secrets to tell, and they love women who just put it all out there, and they love the memes that celebrate being sexual. And, women, let me tell you . . . guys are here for it. I mean, I am. A one-night stand isn't something to be ashamed of—man or woman. Like I said, I diplomatically believe that both men *and* women should put off marriage as long as possible and have as much fun as they possibly can.

Where I come from, there's still an old-school Southern attitude about marriage, which means: Get married at a respectable age (mainly, before forty for guys), have kids, and don't get divorced and shame the family name. My grandmother from Lake Forest, Illinois, asked my mom once if I was gay because I wasn't married by thirty-five years old (obviously gay couples can get married, but like I said, these are old-school attitudes). And I have a friend who married a girl because he was pressured by his traditional Southern dad to "make an honest woman out of her." They ended up being miserable (not because marriage makes everyone miserable, but because they weren't a good match) and they ended up divorcing and disappointing her parents and his. That's why I think traditional marriage is changing—people are saying to hell with the old school, I'm on this planet for a finite number of years, so I choose happiness and freedom over tradition.

I understand that even the best relationships aren't always a walk in the park and there will be tough times, but if those tough times took up 99 percent of the marriage, I would definitely pull the rip cord. Honestly, this has been the crux of my trepidation about marriage and settling down: I don't want to meticulously construct a new life that looks nothing like my current (relatively) stress-free one, only to find that I'm miserable and I have to tear the whole thing down. It's a big risk emotionally, reputationally, and to one's soul. Hurting someone else is terrifying to me. Turning their world upside down, having all their family and friends feel homicidal when your name is mentioned—I just don't want that. It's a disturbance in the Force.

Here's another thing that I've spoken to my therapist about—usually in these situations, the writing is on the wall. But also, what if your family and friends stay close with your ex? I think I read that after Brad Pitt and Jennifer Aniston split up, Pitt's mom and Jennifer remained close and spoke all the time, which gives me hope. It means you don't have to destroy everything in the event of a breakup or a divorce, and that people can (sometimes) remain reasonable. The Aniston-Pitt story doesn't make me want to jump into marriage, but it does ease my fear, just a little.

There's a famous quote by Henry David Thoreau: "Most men live lives of quiet desperation."

That won't be me—I can promise you that.

I'm very lucky that there hasn't been much pressure applied to me by my family in the marriage realm (besides my nana wondering if I was gay). Like I said before, my parents have been together

Graduation day in elementary school. What you don't see here is the teacher privately expressing concern to my mom and dad about my rambunctiousness. *All photos are courtesy of the author.*

As you can see, I took a full swing and hit more tee than ball. What you don't see is that this was a strategy, and it fooled the whole infield. And I reached second base after a string of errors.

My first starring role, as Tigger in our school's production of *Winnie the Pooh*. Little did I know my next line would be in a Bruce Willis movie in 2017.

My sister's high school graduation. I was an early innovator in the selfie game. My little brother was trying to sabotage my shot by holding a branch in front of my face. He paid dearly for his insolence.

Peak awkward years. Notice my ridiculous haircut (pretty sure I cut it myself) and Big Bird–esque stature.

My dad's family has hunting land in South Carolina, and I was taught about the joys of hunting and eating what you kill from an early age.

Yet another installment of peak awkward years. Me and my friend Bailey walking to soccer practice. I hated soccer: Why can't you pick up the ball and run? What is offsides and why? This is probably why they stuck me as goalkeeper.

Sophomore year of high school with my date Lindsey. I was pleased to see she was almost as tall as me.

With my great friend Carter. Believe it or not, I was a cheerleader in high school. I can assure you there were no choreographed dance moves. We pretty much just dressed up and acted outrageous. We came up with wild ways to enter football games, and for this one we commissioned a biker gang to help us show up our rival school.

Me and my bud Jon. I was channeling my inner hippie at this time, which is probably why I got kicked out of boarding school.

With my close boarding school friends. They always made us wear a coat and tie, and we hated it. I cut the sleeves off my nice Oxford shirt because it was so hot.

We almost called this book *The Tooth Hurts*, and this is Exhibit A, around 1996. Definitely not the end of my dental mishaps.

Circa 1997. I'd been kicked out of boarding school and returned to Hilton Head just in time to get an ugly tux, a pretty date, and attend the prom.

Diving in the Bahamas with my family. My vest started to inflate after this photo was taken, so I pushed my little brother into the path of giant beasts to save myself. We never saw him again. But I take solace in the fact that he became part of the ecosystem.

Here I am with my sweet and patient mother, graduating from Hilton Head High School. Wasn't how we drew things up, but even the best-laid plans . . . It all worked out in the end is the important part.

This could be any old summer day growing up on Hilton Head. My friend Scott had a boat, and we cruised and fished and caused mischief pretty much every day.

Summer in Hilton Head, with two of my closest friends, Michael and Andrew. Like I said, all we did was surf, drink, toss the football, and laugh. What an idyllic place.

Before I put my foot in my mouth, I like to dip my shoe in days' old cheese.

With my sister and brother (I was joking about the shark attack). I tried to sabotage every single Christmas card photo, to the point where my mom just embraced the chaos and sent them out.

With three of my best friends in the world. We grew up together, and here we are in 1999 at Red Rocks in Colorado, seeing Widespread Panic.

Dressed as Chuck Norris, probably around 2000. Somehow I found fake chest hair. I wish I still had that American flag kimono. If you've seen it, please return it to me. Shoutout to my friend Matt to my left. He went as a 1980s Chicago businessman.

With my childhood buddy Bailey and college buddy Eric. Georgia was beating Tennessee in football for the first time in a long time. The crowd rushed the field, but we were too drunk to mobilize.

The Tooth Hurts, Exhibit B.

This great shot was taken in Brazil, about an hour from Rio. It was during my study abroad in Buenos Aires, and we basically went surfing and fishing and raised hell—my life story.

Also during my Buenos Aires trip. My family visited, and we went fly fishing in San Martín de los Andes. I was trying to catch a rainbow trout.

When I graduated from college, me and two friends traveled around Southeast Asia for a month. This was in Bali after a long day of good surf.

We were able to score *Sgt. Pepper's* Beatles outfits for Halloween that year. I'm a huge Beatles fan. Props to my friend Bronson for dressing like a fry cook at Waffle House.

One of my early loves, Molly. We were on our way to a horse race, and I guess I needed some TLC.

At my family's mountain house in Linville, North Carolina. I've done so many stupid things that I'm lucky to be here twenty times over, but I sure as hell had fun doing them.

A party at my old house in downtown Charleston, with Kathryn. I always like to see Kathryn walk into a room because I care about her well-being and always enjoy talking to her.

An early batch of Shep Gear hats. My friends have been so supportive, wearing the gear even when they're at a fancy event.

I was contacted by Meals on Wheels, and they told me this sweet lady named Louise was a *Southern Charm* fan, and asked if I would surprise her with a meal. She was shocked, and we had a blast talking. I've been involved with Meals on Wheels since that day.

On *Watch What Happens Live.* Cam and I were probably laughing at Thomas blaming Andy Cohen for making him run for the U.S. Senate.

Craig was nice enough to invite me and a date to this College of Charleston alumni event. This was when Craig and Naomie had just starting seeing each other.

On the set of the Bruce Willis movie *Reprisal.* I played an EMT driver, and Craig played a cop. I had a famous (or infamous) line, but Craig got to throw a shotgun to Bruce, so he won this one.

I'm a big fisherman, but every time we fish on *Southern Charm* it's a disaster. We managed to catch a tiny flounder that somehow felt like a marlin.

This was right before the infamous *Southern Charm* scene where we try to cook ribs for the whole cast. Craig pretends he knows what he's doing, and it becomes a disaster, but it all worked out in the end. We had lots of laughs, and I hope the audience did, too.

Whitney had this explicit and inappropriate cake made for Cam's baby shower. Cam loved it.

Me and Austen feeling no pain on Sullivan's Island.

I've known Chelsea a long time, and it was great having her on the show, although I'm not sure how much she enjoyed it. We'll remain friends forever. She's a great hair stylist, by the way.

Every now and then we get to meet famous people because of the show, and it's usually because Patricia knows them. Here is *Queer Eye for the Straight Guy*'s Carson Kressley. He couldn't have been nicer.

My girlfriend, Taylor, and me in her hometown of Asheville. I jokingly call her "mountain girl" (a subtle Grateful Dead reference), one of many stupid nicknames. I love that she's from the North Carolina mountains. It's a beautiful part of the world and the Southeast, and I have lots of fond memories from that region.

for almost fifty years, so you would think I would have a rosier view of marriage than some. I've never seen my parents get into a serious argument. I'm sure they've had a few, but never around their children. Well, there was this one time when we were in Paris for Thanksgiving when I was thirty-six years old, and my dad was so obnoxiously itinerary-based that everyone was a little on edge. It was me, my parents, plus my brother and sister-in-law, who was pregnant. He wanted us to wake at 7:00 a.m., have breakfast from 8:00 a.m. to 10:00 a.m., the Louvre at 11:00 a.m., then head to Marseille by 2:00 p.m. His meticulous planning took the joy out of many of these wonderful cultural experiences.

Now, there were only so many Clark Griswold jokes we could make before we started to get frustrated with this strict itinerary. My sister-in-law had just discovered that she was pregnant, so she stayed in with my brother most nights, which meant I spent much of my time with my parents—that is, when I wasn't prowling the streets on my own. My mom supported my dad and dutifully went on these excursions, and I ditched them. This was right after the terrible terrorist attacks in Paris, and I said, Fuck museums, I want to walk around the city. It was sobering and enlightening seeing the city at that moment; there were little memorials and flowers in front of the concert venue that was attacked, and I also made it a point to go to the cafés that had been ambushed. As tragic and horrific as it was, it was living history, and the *Mona Lisa* isn't going anywhere. I'm glad I walked the streets instead of staring at some monotonous group of paintings. Once you've seen a thousand paintings, you're usually good. So we all meet back up and it's our last day and my dad breaks out the itinerary and says, "Well, let's have an early dinner because our flight is at nine a.m. and we must leave for the airport at five a.m." This was the last straw! I said under no circumstance would I be leaving that early, and my mom agreed. This was the last straw for Griswold! It was the first time I saw my parents get into an argument, albeit a pretty small one. But what happened next made my heart melt, and it's usually icy cold (although, I do cry in movies literally all the time—see the list following this chapter if you don't believe me). Ignoring my dad's calls for a 5:00 a.m. departure time, we jumped into a taxi and headed to a cool bar I was told about in Paris. My parents weren't speaking because the squabble was fresh, so I sat between them, making jokes and trying to break the ice.

We got to the bar, and as soon as we walked in we were total fish out of water. Well, they were, at least. It was like an old pawnshop turned bar, the kind of place with no sign outside. Inside, it was full of French hipsters, and in stroll my parents looking like Thurston Howell III and his wife (the yacht club couple from. Gilligan's Island, in case the name doesn't ring a bell). The bar actually had little shops and vendors inside of it, and I saw my dad sneak into one of the shops and buy my mom some trinkets as an apology. It was really sweet, and she loved the gifts, and we ended up having a great night.

What my parents showed me that night was that it's very important to keep disagreements private, as much as you can. It's important to not let others know of any internal strife. Besides being tacky as hell to squabble in public (which I know sounds odd coming from someone on *Southern Charm*), it brings others down and can snowball into something bigger. Doing things like taking a deep breath or counting to ten are key, and I assume this is what my parents have mostly always done. My dad's gesture also taught me that whether it's a little trinket at a hipster bar or a watch from Cartier, it means the same thing, and little apologies and gestures and swallowing one's pride are always better than holding a grudge. I'd love to tell you that our Paris story had a happy ending, but that would be a lie. We still got the car at 5:00 a.m. to drive to the airport, and we sat in the terminal unnecessarily for three hours before boarding. My dad had apologized with a trinket, but he still got his way. Not cool, Griswold.

I learned another lesson about love and relationships from my sister. My sister is an amazing person. She's very smart, very even-keeled (well, most of the time), and she's someone I'd trust and confide in until the end of time, so therefore I trust her judgment. She was dating this guy in college everyone loved, and I mean everyone: grandparents, uncles, cousins. Since we all loved him so much, we just figured that was who she'd marry. It all seemed so traditional and it had a family precedent, since my mom was twenty-one years old when she married my dad. Imagine our surprise when my sister broke up with him. How? Why? It had to be one of the hardest things she ever had to do, and I respected the hell out of her for it. She said she simply wasn't in love with him anymore, and she wasn't going to lie to herself or to him or to us about it. If she'd been born twenty or thirty years before, when social pressures were more intense, it would have been a different story. But she had a life to live.

She went to law school, she worked in Washington, D.C., where she started seeing her now husband, she practiced law in New York City for a huge firm, and now she's in Charlotte as in-house counsel for a bank, all while raising three girls. The path of least resistance was never an option for her. Settling wasn't an option. Unlike me, she did end up getting married and having kids, but from her I learned that if you're going to take that plunge into the marital abyss, you better make sure it's with the right person, even if that means breaking it off with someone who, on paper, seems perfect.

I myself wouldn't say I've been all that close to entering into the final frontier that is marriage, even though as I write this, I am seeing a great girl named Taylor. I do think it's a feeling that you have to have. That, or it's time to surrender, which I refuse to do. At least for now. Instead, I'll go surfing when I want and have fun, living in that place between Jeff Bridges and Leo DiCaprio. If I end up a Warren Beatty or a George Clooney, only time will tell. All I know is that I'm not ready to walk the aisle—that I view more as a plank—just yet. Maybe one day soon, though.

Shep's Guide to Dating 101:

Disclaimer: This is the ultimate "do as I say, not as I do" list. I am not a seasoned or serial dater.

1. Girls are just as insecure, clumsy, and desirous to make out as we are. If anyone single is at a bar with friends, chances are they WANT to meet someone.

2. Stay away from Instagram models. Or better yet, the "you can't sit with us" type. They're the sort who are always looking over your shoulder for a better deal.

3. Give everyone a chance, but if someone shows you who they are and you don't like it, don't think change is on the horizon. If someone does a couple of uncool things, you may still be into them, but keep reminding yourself about the things you witnessed.

4. Don't project into the future too much. This is hard to do, and I've fallen prey to it many times. But talking yourself out of something before it happens is very easy but really stupid sometimes. Sounds clichéd, but take it one day/week at a time.

5. Jealousy is a very ugly emotion but can also be a useful tool. I've definitely been a little negligent on a particular night out with a girl I like, and when you look across the room and she's smiling and chatting with another guy it can snap you back into shape. It's a razor's edge, though. Sometimes you have to let your significant other know, like the Beyoncé song says, "Don't you ever for a second get to thinking / You're irreplaceable."

6. Don't juggle girls/boys after two or three months or after you have the "the DTR talk," whichever comes first. It's bad karma and bad for the soul. P.S. I'm sure the time limit

I've given is different for many, but this seems industry standard.

7. Communicate without being annoying. I can't stress this enough. No one is a mind reader. Don't be pissed if you expected an unspoken or implied outcome to go your way and it doesn't.

8. If you are single: Enjoy yourself. You're only young and good-looking once. There's a saying that at age fifty we all get the face we deserve. A shrill and overly guarded person doesn't age well.

9. If you make it so that your happiness is tied to the presence of another person or you make your life all about another person, you're doing life wrong. Being an independent person is the most attractive and important thing you can be.

10. Be honest. All good relationships are based on reciprocity. But it's a rare and beautiful instance where two people feel the same way about each other. If one party senses that the chasm between your feelings is too wide, then be honest. It'll hurt them for a bit, but they'll respect you and you can possibly remain friends. I take pride in not having ill feelings with any of my former girlfriends. My theory is "we spent so many good times together, how could we be mad about it?" But that all hinges on honesty.

11. (In honor of *Spinal Tap*, I'm turning it up to 11). Read books and keep up with the news. Know what's happening in the world. There is nothing more unattractive (to me) than someone who doesn't know who Jeff Bezos is, or who their senators are, or what river the Allies had to cross when they were closing in on Berlin (answer: the Rhine). Also, watch good/funny movies like *Best in Show* and *This Is Spinal Tap*. Like I said, maybe this is just me, but this is my book, so I'm officially enforcing these as strict laws of dating.

Movies
THAT MADE ME CRY

As I've divulged in this chapter, I cry at movies. Often. I am not ashamed. I'm so not ashamed that here is an extensive list of a few that get me every time:

1. *Field of Dreams*: When Costner says, "Hey, Dad, you wanna have a catch," I just break down. Every damn time. I think this is because my dad grew up in Europe and never learned to throw a baseball. Which was fine; my mom threw with me, actually, but she had a terrible arm. Maybe that's why I cry!

2. *Terms of Endearment*: Shirley MacLaine, Jack Nicholson, Debra Winger. I won't reveal too much, but just know you're a monster if you don't cry when you watch this one.

3. *Gandhi*: I was watching this the other night, and when Gandhi starts fasting and his loved ones are pleading with him to eat, I actually looked over and saw my dad well up, and he rarely cries at movies.

4. *Lonesome Dove*: My favorite work of fiction, and a great TV series starring Ricky Schroder (oh, and Robert Duvall, Tommy Lee

Jones, Anjelica Huston, Diane Lane . . .). No spoilers, but let's just say it'll make even the most hard-hearted, burly, stone-faced man cry.

5. *City of God*: A great Brazilian film. Just see it.

6. All right, fine . . . *The Notebook*: Taylor, who I mentioned before, is going to be pissed because she always wants to watch this with me, and I usually avoid it. I was trying to get laid years ago, and I watched this because I thought it might just work as a seduction technique. It didn't, because the poor girl ended up consoling me for half an hour before asking me to leave.

7. *Braveheart*: I cry a few times during this movie, but the big moment is when Mel Gibson cries out "FREEDOM!!!!" It's part sadness, part inspiration.

8. *Weekend at Bernie's*: When Bernie dies and then when he water-skis.

9. *A Beautiful Mind*: When Russell Crowe wins the Nobel Peace Prize and addresses his wife. Heartfelt stuff.

10. *Marley & Me*: Good God, I could not stop at the end.

11. *Up*: The first five minutes had me ugly crying. I know I'm not alone in that.

12. *Legends of the Fall*: When Pitt's dad writes "I am happy" on a chalkboard.

I really could go on and on . . . I'm an emotional movie watcher and book reader, so sue me.

· CHAPTER 7 ·

THE UGLY AMERICAN

Way before I came along, many of my above-average/
exceedingly impressive family members traveled the
world because they were fighting world wars (alongside General
Patton, no less), heading up global corporations overseas, big-game
hunting, or meeting foreign dignitaries. When it comes to traveling (or anything, really), they were all way more accomplished than
yours truly. I was always going to do things differently, though,
so being a below-average progeny doesn't bother me. One of the
benefits of living a life where you're striving for average is a lack of
stress about things that don't matter, like being *above* average.

Even so, I was always inspired by my family members' wild
travel tales. We used to sit around the living room and beg both
of my grandfathers to tell stories about the war, like the times they

withstood a heavy enemy barrage of mortar shells in the Ardennes, or stormed the beaches at Iwo Jima. While I have never stormed the beaches in a dangerous world war, I *have* danced on a beach at Ko Pha Ngan in Thailand until 7:00 a.m. with a guy named Victor and his two Canadian girlfriends! I did it for my country, and for my fellow man.

I'm not trying to brag (really, I'm not), but I'm forty and I've been around the world. And when my dad attempts to regale/impress me with stories about his exploits, whether foreign or domestic, I just have to shake my head. Yes, my relatives traveled, but their adventures were pretty tame. As in "Oh wow, you guys lied and told some girls you had a private plane once at a wedding!" I've literally never been to a wedding where I didn't lie and claim I had a jet, a speedboat, and/or a dune buggy at my disposal. I also bet my dad and his friends never sang Lou Bega's "Mambo No. 5" to a horse in the French Alps and then rode that horse into the hills (bareback!) with the police chief's daughter. I think not! If I recall, her name was Angela, or Pamela, or was it Sandra? Maybe it was Rita? Who knows—what matters is that we had a great time.

My maternal grandfather traveled because of his naval duties. He was on both fronts during World War II, but once his war was won you could barely get him to leave Alabama, let alone the United States. And as much as I love Gramps, I think I'm more like my dad's dad (PaPa) when it comes to exploration. I love seeing different cultures and meeting people in other countries (debauchers, not dignitaries), and as soon as I got a taste of it, travel became a major part of my life. It makes me feel alive and free and all those clichés that are clichés because they're true. On the other hand, I also love having a solid home base—getting back, recharging, sleeping until noon in my own bed at home, and watching movies on the couch all day if the mood strikes. But on occasion, I love to get out of Dodge (by the way, this saying comes from the Old West Kansas town Dodge City, where there was gambling, prostitution, and gunfights. It sounds awesome, but one must "get out" every now and then to maintain sanity). I need to see the world and look for other Dodges, and I guess roaming the globe is in my blood. I like to think my inherent capacity for boredom mixed with my thirst for adventure allows for just the right amount of travel in my life.

My dad and his siblings grew up in Europe because of my grandfather's job as an international manager for Armco Steel, and my dad has a habit of breaking out his fluent Italian whenever he comes across a native. My siblings and I love to tease him whenever we're at an Italian restaurant in a strip mall in South Carolina and he starts speaking the language to order spaghetti. Maybe we make fun of him because we're jealous, which is a confession that should give him a lot of satisfaction. Dammit. You're welcome, Dad.

Because of his experiences, my dad has always been a huge proponent of his kids traveling the world and broadening their horizons. As vast and diverse as America is, you truly become a better person and your appreciation of your own country (sometimes) grows when you see other cultures and meet the locals. Besides, traveling becomes part of your identity. Suddenly at a dinner party you can talk about living in Dubai or Buenos Aires or wherever your travels take you and then you become, like the Dos Equis guy, *the most interesting man in the world*, and you have them right in the palm of your well-traveled hand!

Right this second, I can imagine some of your eyes starting to roll as you say, "Yeah it's easy for you to travel, Shep, and if I had the finances, I would roam the globe, too, asshole . . ." Well, in part you're right. But it's not like I'm staying in five-star resorts and palaces when I travel, and there's always a way to do it cheaply, or cheap-ish. The point is, it's a big world out there, and seeing it should be a priority. At least, it is for me.

Walden writer Henry David Thoreau's big travel experience wasn't overseas, it was to a cabin in Massachusetts, but he wrote:

I went to the woods because I wished to live deliberately, to front only the essential facts of life, and see if I could not learn what it had to teach, and not, when I came to die, discover that I had not lived. . . . I wanted to live deep and suck out all the marrow of life, to live so sturdily and Spartan-like as to put to rout all that was not life, to cut a broad swath and shave close.

This attitude has always resonated with me, as have these lines from another writer hero of mine, Jack Kerouac:

The only people for me are the mad ones, the ones who are mad to live, mad to talk, mad to be saved, desirous of everything at the same time, the ones that never yawn or say a commonplace thing, but burn, burn, burn like fabulous yellow roman candles . . .

Before you roll your eyes, yes I *know* these are some of the most quoted passages in the history of literature and I'm not proving my mental acuity by sharing them here. They're popular for a reason, though, and I like them. Thoreau and Kerouac seem like they were vastly different people, but the goal is the same: to learn more about themselves by experiencing a different reality than most of their peers and fellow citizens. To break the mold. To seek adventures large and small. To drink multiple beers and Jägerbombs with the locals. (Well, maybe not Thoreau.) This resonates with me in so many ways. Yes, I understand that traveling the world isn't as maverick or groundbreaking today as it once was back before Airbnb and Google Maps, and I also understand that very few places are still pristine, since they have been ruined (depending on who you ask) by commercial travel. Even Walden Pond does group tours. That doesn't make travel any less important to *my* life. Which is why I will now regale you with stories of my travels, from the cobblestone streets of South America to the gleaming towers of Dubai. There will be adventure, there will be debauchery, and there will even be occasional enlightenment.

Quick disclaimer: When it comes to travel, or anything else really, I am NOT a role model. So if you're looking for Thoreau-like inspiration or Anthony Bourdain–esque punk rock deep thoughts, please kick off your flip-flops, grab yourself a beer, and settle in for a glimpse of Shepland, on the road. You might not reach enlightenment, but you will have fun.

Side note: Honestly, this chapter is really why I wanted to write this book. I started writing early on in my travels, mainly because some of the stories were so ridiculous, they just had to be shared. So I started emailing all my buddies, and then lightly censoring and sending those emails to my family. Then the emails led to me writing essays. So, included here are a few abridged versions of my travel writing over the years. Maybe one day, when the world (and my mom and dad) are ready, I'll really open the floodgates! For now, here's a taste.

WHEN THE TRAVEL COMES TO YOU

The first indication that my father wanted his children to inherit his wanderlust was the fact that the Roses were VIP members of the local Rotary Club. Because the club is an international service organization, we hosted exchange students as if we were operating a free hostel, except we had air-conditioning and non-communal bathrooms. I suppose it was my parents' way of bringing the culture to us.

I remember having a little trepidation when as a thirteen-year-old I was told that a seventeen-year-old Brazilian was coming to live in our guest room and attend our local high school. My fear quickly disappeared when Fabia entered our lives. She was such a shy, nervous, and ultimately wonderful addition to our family. It also didn't hurt that she was beautiful. I was secretly in love with her. She would babysit me and my prepubescent friends and we'd hang on her every botched English word. She eventually excelled at English and was popular in school and it all worked out great, but she unknowingly broke my heart when she announced that her Brazilian boyfriend, Bruno, was coming to visit. I thought to myself, We'll see about this boyfriend; what does he have that I don't?

Turns out I was very much outmatched because Bruno was a giant hairy man, like a slightly scaled-back, handsome Bigfoot. I'd never seen so much chest hair. He was frolicking around our pool with Fabia all weekend, and I didn't even have pubes yet! It was game over for your boy. My little brother, who was eight years old at the time, used to yell at Bruno because he thought Bruno was hard of hearing, not comprehending that Bruno didn't speak any English. My brother was already an Ugly American at eight years old. If you're unaware, there's an "Ugly American" stereotype that, according to Wikipedia, refers to "American citizens as exhibiting loud, arrogant, demeaning, thoughtless, ignorant, and ethnocentric behavior mainly abroad, but also at home." Despite the Rose family mishaps, I hope Fabia is somewhere out there doing great. She was from Recife, and she regaled us with stories of the beautiful beaches in her home country. Because of her, my appetite for travel was officially whetted.

Next up in our house was Christian from Switzerland. I was going to have an older brother! Our relationship quickly turned into a battle of the wills, though. I think he expected to come in from Europe (from a famously neutral country, no less) and be the alpha rooster in the pen. He was sorely mistaken. We butted heads often, mainly about the TV remote control. I owned that fucking thing, and he aimed to usurp my programming power. What's worse is that all he wanted to do was watch MTV, which wasn't that cool anymore since this was post Mötley Crüe and Bon Jovi, and grunge videos sucked. I also noticed that a pair of my jeans went missing, possibly thanks to Christian. For some reason, kids in Europe were obsessed with blue jeans in the 1980s and early 1990s. I guess the James Dean look took a while to cross the Atlantic. In Christian's defense, he was excellent at mountain biking, which made me a little bitter and jealous. Mountain biking prowess was like currency in my teens. We got into a few little squabbles, but he actually came back to visit a few years later and all we did was laugh about the good times we had, and he didn't steal any denim the second time around. So maybe he *was* like an older brother—you fight like hell, but all you remember is good times.

The third exchange student was actually Christian's little sister (further proof that he enjoyed the experience despite our rivalry . . . or maybe I'm the only one who felt threatened). By the time she came, I had left for boarding school, but by all accounts, she was lovely and easy to live with. Having exchange students live in my childhood home was my first taste of travel. And maybe one of my biggest and most important takeaways from these experiences, other than it helps to be a beautiful Brazilian girl (which is a tough ask for me), was that when you are a stranger in a strange land, you definitely have to treat the situation with a "tread lightly" attitude, at least initially, until you establish yourself as the nut ball you really are. Coming out of the gate hot, personality-wise, can set you back, and it's always best to be respectful. But, as you are about to read, this is another case of do as I say, not as I do! Being respectful in other countries is something I have *tried* to do, but I haven't always accomplished it.

BUENOS AIRES

After my sophomore year in college, I spent the summer in Innsbruck, Austria, with two hundred other American students from various other schools, plus a handful of my buddies from the University of Georgia. We had more fun than should be legal, and in many cases, wasn't. We almost started a riot in Munich (it involved a *biergarten*, a bouncy ball, a scooter, and a McDonald's Happy Meal). We lost our minds on mushrooms dubbed "philosopher stones" in Amsterdam, discovered the wonders of real absinthe in Prague, got ripped off in both London and Budapest (one was a pot deal gone awry, the other a strip club shakedown). I almost had a threesome in Vienna (very Freudian), and we absolutely dominated Italy. Typical Ugly Americans. Not always, but at times, I have fallen soundly into this camp. My college trip around Europe was one of those times. After all, we were college sophomores trying to outdo one another. Still, I usually felt embarrassed by our shenanigans, especially after a brawl with German guys at a disco in Prague when I expertly performed a 360 into a robot on the dance floor, thereby seducing one of their girlfriends (during the melee I mysteriously disappeared with the Fräulein and managed to avoid a physical altercation). All I can say now is that you just have to hope you learn from these mistakes as you grow older, and become a *less* Ugly American as time goes on.

So, after that excursion, I was contemplating whether I should do one more jaunt overseas before I was out of college and I was expected to have a job (or at least a plan). College abroad is itself a "plan," right? Nobody thinks you are slacking off or partying with fellow revelers; they think you are studying and broadening your intellectual horizons! Fools! The brilliant part, and the part I'm eternally grateful for, is that I was heartily encouraged by my parents to be as bold in my travels as possible. When my dad and I sat down to talk about the possibility of spending a senior year semester abroad, it wasn't should I . . . It was: *Where* should I?

I was fearful that the entire continent of Europe was still feeling the reverberations of my previous blitzkrieg, plus I was pretty sure Interpol had a file on me, so I started to look southward. I found a program in Buenos Aires, Argentina. My dad happily approved, since he had spent some time down there fishing and hunting, and he described the city as "cosmopolitan, beautiful, historic, a real knockout." I was sold.

My dad was spot-on. It was an amazing city. Also noteworthy is that this was going to be my first time traveling alone. All of a sudden, I was like the exchange students who lived with my family all those years before, except I had my own apartment with three other guys in the heart of Recoleta, which is a fancy neighborhood in downtown Buenos Aires. The city is divided into numerous little eclectic neighborhoods, sort of like New York City. Palermo is artistic and hipster, Puerto Madero is a cool spot near the port with the best steak restaurant in South America, called Las Lilas. Then there is the gritty but cool La Boca, and then the super-posh country club suburbs called San Isidro (to name a few).

But back to my lodging . . . Looking back I sort of wish I had opted to stay with a family, but the program, which was through NYU, offered for me to stay with fellow students in the French ambassador's apartment in what is the equivalent of Midtown Manhattan. I guess the French ambassador thought it was an altruistic thing to do, or maybe they got a tax break. Either way, it sounded pretty good to me, and the apartment was nicer than any place I'd lived in college, by a mile. Plus, judging by the state I was in when I stumbled home late every night, a wholesome family might have had a serious case of buyer's remorse with me in their house. I might have tainted their impression of the entire continent of North America.

I showed up to the program this preppy-looking kid from the American South, surrounded by a bunch of NYU students who were a little more seasoned when it came to the fast-paced city life. Still, I think they initially underestimated me. They thought I was right off the turnip truck. But it wasn't long before I was leading the charge into some crazy situations and fearlessly tickling the seedy underbelly of Buenos Aires. After getting to know who the other ne'er-do-wells were in the group (I have a solid radar for this, as you might imagine), we took the city by storm. Or maybe it was the other way around? Anyway, shit got real.

I met a contact at a cool little bar, a handsome blond dude—let's call him Hans—who always wore a scarf, back before scarves became hipster cool. Hans knew everything happening in the city, and he became our underground debauchery tour guide. If you need a more intricate mental picture of this dude, he walked around with a pet monkey on his shoulder, right next to his scarf. I forgot the monkey's name, so I'll just call it Bubbles. Anyway, we went to a handful of good spots on his suggestion but the granddaddy of them all was a club called Pacha. It opened at midnight and closed whenever it wanted. I knew nothing of world-famous DJs at the time, but years later I discovered they were all playing there (Paul Oakenfold comes to mind). It was an amazing scene. The whole place was pulsating, and there I was, a twenty-one-year-old from University of Georgia, just dancing and doing other normal activities, like running full speed into chain-link fences (an early attempt at trying to get a laugh) and falling backward as a small crowd yelled *"La American!"*

My nights in Buenos Aires with Hans and Bubbles included VIP booths where Diego Maradona (basically the Michael Jordan of soccer) strolled in at 4:00 a.m., while the whole club chanted "Diego!" One night a cute Argentine girl told us to come out to the country with her at 7:00 a.m., and who was I to refuse? I jumped on a party bus with a bunch of strangers and found myself at a massive house in San Isidro with music blaring inside. It was like I was in a dream state—and what a dream! We walked around the hedges to the party to find topless girls swimming laps in the pool, while people danced all over the lawn. Somehow, I eventually made it home, and because it was all so dreamlike, I'm actually not sure what was real and what I imagined.

I also have a distinct memory of one crazy night at the U.S. ambassador's house. I had met his daughter out on the town and had been invited to a party at their home (they were out of town—

beer bash at the ambassador's house!). There was security every-where, plus a lot of cool expats and English-speaking locals. I met a beautiful Mexican American gal who had just graduated from Princeton, and we hit it off immediately. I've always done well with Ivy League women—my pseudo-intellectualism and irrational con-fidence work like a charm . . . though eventually I'm exposed as the ne'er-do-well that I am. Before this Princeton lass discovered the real Shep, we had a little rendezvous in the coat closet of the ambas-sador's house before ending up at her place, which was a balling-ass apartment. She had a wet bar full of top-shelf liquor, so there I was frolicking around in satin sheets drinking Maker's Mark, neat. It was like a Madonna video. The next morning, I decided to float/walk home, which was at least a couple of miles, and I came across a Hooters franchise! I thought it fitting that I waltz in and sample a platter of their finest appetizers, washed down with a cold Sprite. It's another moment I'll never forget, sitting in a Hooters with a postcoital glow in the middle of Buenos Aires.

Another adventure took me to Rio de Janeiro for a week, and what a time that was. If hazy memory serves, I made out with approximately eight beautiful Brazilian girls on the dance floor in one night (thereby satisfying my exchange student Fabia fixa-tion). Unfortunately, all eight make-out sessions ended right there on the dance floor, since Catholicism reigned supreme and these girls typically lived with their parents until they were married. The same was true in Buenos Aires—you'd always see young people just hard-core sucking face on a park bench or on the street for hours at a time. Thanks for the cockblock, Catholicism.

In addition to respectfully sucking face with the local girls, it's always nice to immerse yourself in a culture and learn a new language. But, in keeping with the Ugly American stereotype, I barely learned any Spanish while I was in Argentina. I truly believe that linguistics is an innate talent. Some people are born with that talent, and I'm not one of them. One of my Buenos Aires friends was amazing at languages. He lived in Greece for one summer and not only did he learn that language—he also picked up Swiss German from one of his roommates. What a dick. When we traveled together, I would lean on him to get my point across to the locals. My inherent impatience coupled with my ability to use linguistically talented friends as a crutch led to my very rudimentary understanding of Spanish. To be good at languages, you have to be totally unselfconscious, and be willing to fail spectacularly. I guess I just had trouble with that. Plus, you have to have a really good ear for it, and let's face it, I'm not the best listener in the world, as any woman I've dated could probably tell you. But I will say that there is a level of osmosis in language that embeds itself in your mind, whether you realize it or not. So, if I spend a few days in a Spanish-speaking country, I find myself starting to speak a little, which always catches me off guard. The problem comes when I'm in a non-Spanish-speaking country and I've had a couple of drinks and I just start speaking Spanish, which is confusing to most, as you can imagine.

Besides the wine, women, and Hooters pit stops, one of my favorite parts of traveling is correspondence. Instead of handwritten letters, I write emails, and many of my emails are sent with the intention of tormenting my parents, who are sitting at home, worrying about me. To give you a taste, here is an email I sent my mom before I returned from Buenos Aires, in accordance with the long-standing tradition of trying to rile her up:

Mother, I'll be home soon, and I would be less than forthright if I didn't reveal the fact that I come to you a new man! No more alcohol or sedatives in my life. No more late nights carousing and consorting with floozies and ne'er-do-wells. From now on it's a sensitive/selfless Shep who will be tiptoeing down your halls. Who knows what has driven me all these years to howl at the moon and piss in the wind, though whatever it was I was looking for or hoping to satiate, I've found here in Argentina! That's right, I've found my calling: The omnipresent Catholic church here has shown me the way. I want to be a man of the cloth. A Priest! I figure, first I ask for a heaping helping of forgiveness, then I start looking at seminaries, maybe wander back to old North Quaker Lane* in Virginia. Oh God in Heaven I am prepared to go the extra mile for you and your domain!

Love Shep
P.S. Please write in your calendar an appointment for me to get a new driver's license. Mine is lost and I'd hate to go searching for my maker without proper identification!

---

* Site of my old boarding school.

I ended up spending six months in Buenos Aires, longer than I'd spent anywhere else without family and friends. But the amount of new friends I made was amazing, and the things I saw and the cultural experiences I had were unforgettable (even Hooters). It's eye-opening being so far removed from what you know. Seeing how others live helps open your mind and helps you sympathize with the plight of others. Brace yourself, because I'm going to get a little political here despite my better judgment, but traveling can help you understand why people risk their lives in a caravan trying to get to the U.S. because their dictator leader hoards their resources and persecutes their freedoms. You become empathetic.

Besides the empathy and nightclubs and topless women, my biggest takeaway of the trip was studying under all these Argentine professors who had very different versions of how world events took place than your garden-variety American textbook would show. Napoleon once said, "History is a set of lies people have agreed upon," and I wholeheartedly agree. In Argentina I also went to a rally against government corruption, and some local students suggested that I leave the protest because violence was in the air. I think in some ways that experience fortified my distrust of authority. This trip was also the first time I'd ever met an openly gay person. He was a student at NYU, and he was actually one of my three roommates. I mean, I'm sure I had met gay people in the past, but being from the South at that time, they didn't come right out and say it. My roommate was fun to talk to, smart, snarky—he possessed all of my favorite qualities. So that was a cool part of opening my mind to that world as well, and I have traveling to thank for that.

DUBAI

As I said earlier in this book, between your first and second year of business school you are expected to get a summer internship. Most of my comrades were interested in investment banking or finance, so naturally a lot of Wall Street and hedge fund opportunities were high on their list. Others wanted to do the corporate thing. I remember a few people interned at Walmart, headquartered in Benton, Arkansas, which is—wait for it—a fucking dry county! No, thanks, guys. I wanted to try something truly unique (in a place where you could freely buy beer at all times) and feed the adventurous spirit that my dad instilled in me.

So I came up with a plan to leverage relationships I forged through my last employer (the golf legend/entrepreneur Greg Norman) and see if I could get on board with an operation somewhere cool and different, somewhere that had culture and cocktails. I think we can all agree that I accomplished this by securing that internship in Dubai I mentioned, during the summer of 2008. Dubai was one of the fastest-growing and most extravagant cities in the world at that time (they had pretend ski slopes inside of malls, self-proclaimed seven-star hotels, and $200 cocktails, to give you a mental picture). I managed to somehow get my ducks in a row with the company, which was incidentally and brilliantly called Leisurecorp (after all, leisure is my specialty).

So I landed in Dubai one sunny day in June. Actually, every day is sunny and brutally hot, but no one likes talking (or reading) about the weather, so let's move on.

A guy picked me up from the airport in a BMW 740 and drove me to the hotel, which was a Holiday Inn Express in a part of Dubai called—wait for it—Internet City! The service at the hotel was prompt. The Leisurecorp office was full of cool people from Egypt, Iran, the U.K., and Australia, so I brought the South Carolina culture to the mix, I guess. Everyone was constantly ribbing each other, so I fit right in, since that is a favorite pastime of mine. They also all smoked, so I contemplated becoming a chain smoker so they'd invite me to parties. Their sales record was through the roof, totaling somewhere around $300 million in two weeks, so no wonder everyone was in such a good mood.

I had gotten a taste of this in Buenos Aires, but it really hit home in Dubai: When you're traveling, stereotypes tend to melt away since you get to actually talk to so many people from different cultures or backgrounds. The stakes became a little higher for me in Dubai, not just because I was trying to map out my future, but because there wasn't a lot of room for error, behaviorally, which was a tightrope walk for me, as you can probably imagine. I figured out pretty quickly that I probably shouldn't start brawls or drunkenly run headlong into fences or dumpsters in the Middle East. I was fearful that an uncool gesture might get me incarcerated, so I walked on eggshells a little bit and prayed that this wisdom and cautiousness would stick after a Johnny Walker or three.

I met so many amazing people in Dubai, from the bartender at my Holiday Inn Express who would call my room to tell me that he had a cold beer waiting for me so I would come down and watch soccer with him, to my driver Samir, who called me "Sef" and picked me up in some outrageous locations (often along with several lovely flight attendants). Samir constantly asked me to go out drinking with him, and at the end of the summer I bought him a pair of sunglasses as a parting gift, and we were literally saying goodbye in tears! There were the two Iranian women I bonded with immediately (one was a pop star stuck selling real estate, the other the sweetest gal in the world). I could hear anguish in their voices when they talked about how scary the Middle East could be if you were gay or a critical thinker or an artist, but they also said that despite all that, they stayed because they wanted to break out of the fundamentalist tendencies and change things however they could. We had a momentary connection in a foreign place, and talking to them changed my perception of what I thought I knew, and taught me a valuable lesson not to judge anything or anyone until you dig a little deeper. This goes for any subject, person or culture. And even then, try to keep an open mind. See, travel can make even the most rambunctious Ugly American into a great philosopher!

But don't worry—I didn't shed my Ugly American–isms entirely. In Dubai I also fell in with a group of scalawags, wannabes, dark horses, also-rans, underdogs, nuevo riche, viejo riche, and straight players (I was of the latter). I met them through work, at clubs, and about town. It also turned out that my company (can a lowly intern say "my company"?) employed models several times a year for different functions, and these gorgeous women basically served as greeters and equity partners (kidding, again). I never had luck with any of the models (though I tried), but I did meet a stunner from Bulgaria at a beach bar one night. Her name was ZZ (as in Top, but not). She asked me if I even knew where Bulgaria was and although I had no idea at the time, I said, "Yeah, isn't that an old Russian province where they make caviar?" Needless to say, she was not impressed, but after some posturing and playing crowd favorite "Cheap Sunglasses" by the *actual* ZZ Top on the jukebox, I landed a make-out session, and we had a rapturous one-month long Dubai affair.

ZZ and I had a great time, but as all romances go (at least in Shepland) it had to end, and soon. One weekend I guess I basically ignored her because I was busy chasing other gals around Dubai. In response to my antics, she sent me an email, a few lines of which I'll share with you now:

I wish you were different, a little warmer. You will be one day, I am sure. I just do not have the willingness to play games or waste my time.

I think ZZ really touched on some pertinent details of my psyche, so I see her email as very useful constructive criticism. Not that I've changed all that much since then, but still. ZZ must not have been that angry, because she later said that she wanted to come visit me in the U.S. because (in a sexy Eastern European accent), "I have never met anyone quite like you." Alas, it never happened. I guess we'll always have Dubai.

On my trip, I also became friends with a guy named Saif whose dad was a doctor for the royal family in the United Arab Emirates. One of the first things Saif said to me was "What's mine is yours!" And what was his was an amazing house on a man-made island shaped like a palm tree (not kidding, his house was on one of the "fronds"), complete with an infinity pool and a private beach. He would throw parties with fifty people drinking and playing volleyball, free styling (swimming, not rapping), beer bonging, belly flopping, kayaking, ultimate Frisbee–ing, swan diving, and engaging in general tomfoolery. And I know I said that I tried to be on my best behavior in the Middle East, but I did manage to wake up one morning with a good old-fashioned MARI (mysterious alcohol-related injury) that happened when I drunkenly tackled a trash can the night before. The trash can did have a dent in it, so we'll call it a draw.

So, while I didn't entirely shed my Ugly American tendencies in Dubai, I did experience life in the Middle East, I met amazing people from all over the world, and I expanded my horizons, culturally and personally. I did manage to leave Dubai with the promise of a lucrative full-time job when I finished business school, but in keeping with my reputation as someone who likes to lower the bar, things didn't quite pan out that way. . . .

HONG KONG

When I left Dubai with the promise of a future job, life was GOOD! I finally had my ducks in a row! Perhaps I was going to be above average after all!

Soon after my trip, though, the economy came crashing down and the crisis of 2008 wiped out not just my prospects, but the prospects of hundreds of thousands of people. The party was officially OVER, and little by little I started to realize that my chances of success in Dubai were rapidly eroding.

The first indication was that nobody at Leisurecorp was answering my phone calls. I was finally able to get through to one of my buddies at the company, and they confirmed my fears: The money was gone, people were pulling out of deals left and right, and foreign investment (which fueled the city) had completely dried up. People were fleeing the city to go back to Britain or the U.S. or wherever, abandoning their Range Rovers in the airport parking lot because they were in such a rush to get the hell out. My friend simply said, "Mate, it'll be a miracle if any of us have a job here . . . it's game over."

I was back to square one, or, really, square negative one. My classmates and I were going to graduate business school in maybe the worst possible time in U.S. history. Nobody had a job lined up. So it was back to good old Hilton Head Island for me—an unceremonious return, but a beautiful place to regroup and figure out my next plan. The plan took a while to formulate, but the good news is that I had lots of friends in the golf business and I was able to get my handicap down to a 4.5 because I played every day. As exciting as that was, though, it wasn't going to validate my business school education (not quite like reality TV has!).

So my dad sat me down and said I was going to have to think outside the box and maybe turn over some stones that I hadn't thought about. I agreed, and he came up with a plan. For some reason he was under the impression that Hong Kong hadn't been hit as hard as some of the other major financial city centers, and that I should go out there and poke around a bit. Sold! So I took a gamble and went to go look for a job on the other side of the world during one of the worst global economic recessions in history. Tallyho!

On my first day in Hong Kong I got up at 6:00 a.m., ready to conquer the world and become a new man. Actually, I got up because my internal clock was scrambled from traveling; I had no intention of becoming a responsible adult right out of the gate. I walked around the quiet early-morning streets to get my first real breakfast in years—if you don't count my mom making me cereal at 10:30 a.m. when I would wake up (actually, better make that 11:00 a.m.). After breakfast I decided to do a little exploring, and within an hour the city had come alive. It was a pretty cool transformation, full of busy markets and stores, and I wandered through a wild area full of bars that reminded me of Bourbon Street in New Orleans. I also found a gay S&M store called Gentleman's Agreement, thereby proving my theory that most gay men have an amazing sense of humor (see my well-researched list of my favorite gay bar names on the next page).

Favorite Gay Bar Names:

1. The Hung Jury

2. The Man Hole

3. Moon Jammers

4. Bone Shakers

5. Up in Adam (This one is actually the name of the gay brunch spot I dream of opening.)

While I went to Hong Kong to land a job, I made sure to reserve plenty of time to wake up next to beautiful women in random hotel rooms, get drunk with locals and expats and fellow travelers, and engage in general (and not so general) revelry. At one exclusive club, the bouncer told me it was members only, so I asked if he would accept a member of the South Carolina Yacht Club. Somehow, it worked! The bar was jam-packed with gorgeous women and male model, Zoolander-type guys. I spent two fruitless hours at the bar, engaging in encounters like this:

Me: You want to take a shot?!
Girl: I don't speak English (in perfect English).

Or:

Me: Hey, man, how's it going? There's some awfully hot girls here.
Dude: Yeah, there are . . . are you with any of them?

Me: Nope . . . but we should act like we belong so as not to scare them off.
Dude: I do belong . . . I'm a male model.

One night out I met a waitress at a hotel bar. I invited her to my place, but her friend was the biggest wet blanket in history and was blocking me big-time. Lucky for me, my girl was persistent and she insisted that I come with them. I figured we would walk a little ways to her place, but we got on a bus and started commuting to who knows where. About thirty minutes later, we were in the middle of nowhere. *And then we get off the bus and get into a cab!* Was I being kidnapped? I asked where we were going, and she said to her parents' place. Shit.

So we get to a tiny apartment and go into her cubicle-size, single-bed room. At this point I was completely geographically confused, but there *was* a bed there, so I soldiered on, had a great time, and then we fell asleep. In the morning, I heard some rumbling outside, *and then her mom walked in*! I played dead while my girl and her mom said God knows what to each other outside the room, in heated tones. I quickly contemplated jumping out of the window, but to my dismay it was twenty-six stories high! I decided to stay quiet and observe her room. She was obsessed with Scotland for some weird reason, and there were pictures of shirtless guys wearing kilts lining her bedroom walls. Maybe she took me home because she thought I was some sort of Nordic conqueror. She also had an impressive Japanimation doll collection that I took selfies with while she fought with her mom, who

SHEP ROSE

occasionally peered in to see the half-naked American giant in her daughter's tiny room. I pulled the blanket up to my chin and prayed for the madness to end. Eventually, once her parents calmed down and left for work, I was able to leave not out the window, but the front door. I never saw her again. Frankly, I was a little pissed she got me into that situation and I wasn't eager to revisit it.

In between trying (sort of) to secure gainful employment in Hong Kong, I also hooked up with a Texas girl named Amber who I liked mainly because she listened to all my stories and didn't interject with annoying questions. I also met an Indian guy named Sven who seemed to have stockpiled all of the cocaine in Asia in his plush apartment. Amber and I went to underground clubs with Sven and his friends, the kinds of clubs that have actual shark tanks inside of them. I arranged via Sven to allow Amber to feed squid to the sharks (always a good idea to allow drunk, coked-out foreigners access to apex predators). I also loved the bathroom graffiti I saw in these clubs, and I'm actually obsessed with the idea of creating a coffee table book of bathroom graffiti from around the world. I wrote one memorable example from Hong Kong in my journal at the time:

Sex is like math: You add the bed, subtract the clothes, divide the legs, and pray you don't multiply.

Other bathroom graffiti I love:

1. Is she the one or one of the ones?

2. Is she Ms. Right or Ms. Right Now?

3. Our butt cheeks touched the same surface. We are brothers. We are one!

4. Your mom is a nice lady and your father is proud of you.

5. Here I sit, brokenhearted. Came to shit, but only farted.

6. Roses are tits/Violets are tits/I love tits/Tits tits tits.

7. The future is in your hands. Your dick is the future.

Before you cancel me for being insensitive/immature/gross/misogynistic/unevolved, understand that I'm just the messenger here, but I do think it would make a cool book. Maybe it was all the bathroom scrawls, but during my Hong Kong trip I started getting an itch to write, so I actually sent one of my journal entries to *Esquire* magazine to see if they wanted to publish it. Here's the intro email that I sent:

I'm an unemployed MBA graduate who recently spent 16 days in Hong Kong looking for work and having other various misadventures. I'm not sure if you guys at Esquire *are at all interested, but I kept a journal of my travels and there's some pretty funny material within. I'll paste a sample for*

*your enjoyment (or repugnance). If you like it, let me know.
I have lots more.*

Shep Rose

Now, many of you may be wondering: Wasn't Shep supposed to be looking for a job this whole time? And yes, you're right, that was the goal. And honestly, I tried. In between clubs and horse races and frolicking with beautiful women, I met with a guy at an internet start-up that was downsizing (sweet!). I also met some very nice expats who were in the commercial real estate game there. I talked to a finance guy, but predictably he said the market was upside down and unless you'd been there a while and had people in the company in your corner, you were screwed. So basically, I was screwed.

One day, to take a break from networking and partying, I decided to hike up to Victoria Peak, which is the highest hill in the area, with panoramic views of Hong Kong and the bay surrounding it. There's a tram that takes tourists up, but I was told the hike is sort of cool. It actually almost killed me. It wasn't that it was so grueling, but there was virtually no signage, so I would go up five hundred yards vertically, then hit a dead end. Once I got to the top, exhausted but also exhilarated, I was expecting at most a little gift store, or maybe one quaint bodega. To my surprise there was a Burger King, a McDonald's, a Bubba Gump Shrimp, plus a few other little shops and restaurants. I guess Forrest Gump ran all the way to Hong Kong.

While I was there, I had a travel-induced epiphany that changed the course of my life, or at least started to. I saw a group of guys in suits and ties, all sitting on a park bench, hunched over laptops and looking stressed and miserable. They must have been having a meeting or something, but as I watched those guys, I suddenly realized that the corporate, suit-and-tie life was not for me. All the jobs I'd been trying to land were not for me! In that moment I thought, *Fuck putting on a suit and looking at numbers all my life.* I wanted to be a twenty-first-century version of a conquistador or a pirate and somehow cobble together a living and just burn, baby, burn, like Jack Kerouac and Hemingway. I had been writing all these emails and journals, so I thought, maybe I could write? After my excursion, I headed to the horse races and lost every bet I placed, but I had a damn good time in the process.

Hong Kong was a dead end career-wise, but socially it was a win, which brings me to a theory I've formulated over the years. My dad was always advising me to go somewhere for a few weeks and try to lock down a job and then return to Hong Kong when things were set. I tried this in San Francisco, Dubai, and Hong Kong, and it never worked out. So my advice is this: If you are interested in a region or city, just fully commit and move there. Get your feet on the pavement and take a risk. I remember one final meeting I had with a successful businessman who knew my god-father. We had a wide-ranging, passionate discussion about politics and culture and travel, and it was great. But when I left his ornate high-rise office and headed back into the streets of Hong Kong, I slapped my forehead because I had completely forgotten to ask this guy about jobs! Still, I wouldn't have changed one second of our meeting, and as Forrest Gump and his mom would agree, it was fate. I wasn't meant to live in Hong Kong. After all, I had a reality TV show that was waiting for me in the near future. . . .

William S. Rose III
sheprose@gmail.com
93 Harbour Passage
Hilton Head Is., S.C.
Cell - 843 422 6135

EDUCATION

VANDERBILT UNIVERSITY   Nashville, Tn.
OWEN GRADUATE SCHOOL OF MANAGEMENT
Master of Business Administration, May 2009
Concentration: Real Estate and Finance
GPA: 3.4

UNIVERSITY OF GEORGIA   Athens, Ga.
Bachelor of Arts May 2002
Major: Economics
GPA: 3.1

NEW YORK UNIVERSITY   Buenos Aires, Argentina
Spring 2001 - Argentina abroad program
• Completed courses in South American history, economics and political science

EXPERIENCE

ASSET MANAGEMENT ASSOCIATES INC.   Hilton Head Is., S.C.
2009   *Consultant*
• Located distressed properties in the U.S. in order to make bids on them. Helped prepare proposal to investment funds for purchasing distressed properties.

LEISURECORP INC. (A subsidiary of Dubai World)   Dubai, UAE
2008   *Summer Intern*
• Worked in the Transactions Department. Created models to analyze properties and conducted feasibilities for real estate investment opportunities around the world.
• Wrote investment memorandums that were read by senior management.

ASSET MANAGEMENT ASSOCIATES INC.   Hilton Head Is., S.C.
2007   *Marketing Consultant*
• Created powerpoint presentations and several real estate marketing materials promoting commercial properties valued at over $30 million.
• Initiated a web page design for a master planned property complete with local statistics, aerial photos, and comparable sales in the area.
• Analyzed investment opportunities in the Savannah, Georgia and Hilton Head, South Carolina. Established a spreadsheet model that estimated construction, marketing, legal costs, etc. along with sales forecasting to find an IRR for the investment.

MEDALLIST DEVELOPMENTS INC. (A subsidiary of Macquarie Bank, Australia)   Jupiter, Fl.
2004-2006   *Market Analyst*
• Integrated the first in-house marketing and research department for the company.
• Used economic trends to advise management where to purchase land. Subsequently, the company contracted for land in excess of $70 million in the areas that I recommended.
• Traveled to different locations as part of a "swat team" to collect data and establish local contacts.
• Produced a quarterly U.S. housing industry report for Macquarie Bank executives.
• Member of investment proposal team. Constructed numerous detailed requests for debt and equity to develop new projects.

DIVOSTA HOMES INC. (A subsidiary of Pulte Homes)   West Palm Beach, Fl.
2003-2004   *Market Analyst*
• Worked in the segmentation department of the large homebuilder, studied local markets and fellow competitors such as D.R. Horton and KB Homes in order to discover sales trends in the area.
• Assisted in the production of a yearly market report that was presented to the CEO of Pulte Homes.
• Trained analysts to collect and interpret data.

My grossly exaggerated résumé from this era. Half of these jobs involved me stocking snacks or planning lunches, all to great acclaim.

COSTA RICA

Right before the first season of *Southern Charm* was set to start filming, I was gearing up to move from Hilton Head to Charleston to start this new crazy life/experiment of being on reality TV. I had no clue where the show would lead (hell, most of us figured it would run for a few episodes and then just fade away), and I wanted to get out of town, clear my head, catch some waves, and see what Central America had to offer. I had also just ended my four-month-long relationship with Danni from *Southern Charm*, and I felt like I needed to start fresh, and surfing and relaxing in Costa Rica seemed like just the way to do it.

But there was more to it than that. Ever since my epiphany in Hong Kong, the one where I realized that a life of corporate drudgery wasn't for me, I was still secretly harboring that desire to write. I wanted to be a travel writer in the spirit of the great gonzo journalist himself, Hunter S. Thompson, or even Ernest Hemingway. Lofty goals for someone who touts lowering the bar, I know. But I started to notice that my creativity exploded whenever I was a stranger in a strange land. Couple that with the fact that I was willing to unflinchingly put myself in dangerous or tenuous situations, all in the name of fun or "living deliberately" or "burning bright," if you will. Actually, my desire to write started way back in Buenos Aires, but, in keeping with my "do as little as possible and have fun" motto, I wasn't diligent about actually taking time to write.

In any case, I bet I could find interesting miscreants if you dropped me in the middle of the Sahara (I'd befriend the coolest, or shall I say hottest, Bedouins in the desert). So I went to Costa Rica intent on writing about my experience and seeing whether I actually liked writing, or if I was any good at it. It turns out I liked it a lot. I actually wrote a 9,000-word essay about the trip and submitted it to various publications like *Surfer's Journal* and *Esquire*, but I guess people weren't ready for my idiocy (or for a 9,000-word essay). Their loss! I guess rejection is part of being a real writer, so in that sense my literary baptism was a success.

For your entertainment, here's a piece of that essay:

Week 1

My first impression is that this place is right out of a Hunter S. Thompson novella, and I am not exaggerating. I am no spring chicken. I have lived and debauched in Buenos Aires, Prague, Munich, Hong Kong, Dubai, Thailand, and various other places. But this place is absolutely anything goes. It appears to be completely lawless. The Dodge City of Central America.

First let me explain why I decided to come here for a month, or at least why I wanted to come here. The country of Costa Rica's slogan, which one can find on an endless amount of hats, shirts, and bumper stickers, is "Pura Vida" which translates to "Pure Life." So that is my plan. To surf with hometown friends for eight days, stay for 20 more, try to improve my Spanish, to live healthily and relax. It turns out I was being optimistic . . .

Like I wrote back then, my intention was to live clean (daily beers being part of that regimen), go to bed early, surf every morning, write in my journal, and basically kind of unplug and "slow down." When I reached the beach town Malpais, which is about a five-hour car and ferry ride from the capital, San Jose, I did manage to slow down, for about five minutes. Once I realized that I was surrounded by a bunch of locals, expats, and travelers who were out to raise hell, I was along for the ride. On night one, I found myself out partying at warp speed until the early morning, but I *did* decline a 2:30 a.m. offer of ecstasy pills from some French revelers, so in a sense maybe I was slowing down? (Oh, let's face it, I just wanted to get up early and surf on my first morning . . . otherwise I probably would have been climbing trees in the jungle at dawn).

Another observation from my essay:

Everything down here is slow and shifting, like a sandbar . . . If you live in Costa Rica for an extended period of time, you're going to have lots of down time, time alone, time for reflection. There's no Seinfeld reruns, air-conditioned living rooms, bowling alleys, and other little ways to mindlessly kill time in Costa Rica. So, you might as well slow down and make your little jaunt up the coast to find waves an all-day affair. There's no point in rushing there or rushing back. Take your time; don't ask for the check at lunch right when you're done, embrace silence and inactivity . . .

In Costa Rica I discovered a place where time is relative. Eventually I got into a rhythm where I did slow down a little bit. I surfed in the mornings, played a lot of Ping-Pong, ate amazing food, wrote in my journal every day, and met interesting people with names like "Medicated Jay." I also hooked up with a Costa Rican girl who started referring to me as "Shepito" (little Shep) to her friends, and I remain blissfully and willfully ignorant about the potential negative connotations of that nickname. It was surreal telling my new friends in Costa Rica that I was about to be on TV while we were floating in the ocean, eating papayas, and drinking beers on the beach. I had no clue then what *Southern Charm* would become. Like I said, I thought it would be a flash in the pan. Obviously, I was wrong.

Anyway, surfing is really the best natural high I've ever experienced, producing a state of bliss I can only imagine would be akin to waking up next to a Victoria's Secret model. The first week was about going with the flow, and I really started to feel said flow. Here's an excerpt from the second week:

Week 2

This place is really starting to win me over, slowing down is becoming a revelation and almost my new mantra (can't believe I just typed that). I'm quick not to blur my new mantra with the simple practice of laziness, or at least I'm careful not to. Truth is, there is a lot of "Mañana" attitude here. But slowing down to me is directly correlated to exercising patience, of which I arrived here with little. It is however a very impor-

tant and valuable trait to possess and I intend to bask in its
perceived glow.

Then my Ugly American side came back to me like a comfort-
ing warm blanket . . . or ceiling fan in this case (it was hot as fuck
there):

Later during Week 2 . . .
   The maxim "Slow Down" is starting to piss me off. I tried
to accomplish a few errands today, which proved to be a
near impossible task. I wanted to buy a beach cruiser and
get a pair of sunglasses. However, I'm stuck in the land of
SLOW DOWN. Nobody is very helpful, encouraging, or
motivated. Slowing down is starting to seem like a euphe-
mism for procrastination and plain old laziness. Most sug-
gestions are met with "we'll see" or "sounds cool, I'll think
about it." I'm trying to stay patient, but it's becoming dif-
ficult. I want to explore and go someplace new, even if it's
down the street. I managed to find the sunglasses, which
feels like a major accomplishment. Looks like the bike will
have to put off for another day, again. This procrastination
also contaminated my attempt to get good at Spanish. I had
lived in Buenos Aires for six months several years ago and
wanted to start formally learning the language again. The
teacher in town delayed our first meeting three times over a
two-week period, so I just gave up. It was disheartening but
hardly surprising.

There were ebbs and flows.

Nearing Week 6 . . .

As my trip concludes, I've realized how versatile Costa Rica is and I never even really left one town. It's really up to you—choose your own adventure. Free Will can be a great source of pride or the most dangerous of foes. Maybe there is no location or destination in the world that automatically puts you on a good, healthy and righteous path. But Costa offers all kinds of choices, and everything is out there for the taking. There are volcanos, rainforests, you name it. All interesting and wondrous places that I didn't even come close to seeing!

I have confidence in my affability, but as you can see, even I, the benevolent dictator of life of Shepland, found it hard to retain the "Slow Down" attitude forever. Eventually I wanted to get back to "normal" life, the one where I might not be able to surf every morning, but I also don't have to wait fifteen hours for a bus. But the best version of Shepland is the one where I take it international, and Costa Rica was the perfect place for that. Out of the country I become more introspective, and I morph as appropriately as I can to fit the place I'm in. There's nothing rote about it. Everything becomes new and filled with wonderment, and there's a level of childlike innocence that I revert back to. It's glorious.

That desire to write stayed with me, and was ignored by the professionals at the time (damn you, *Esquire!*), but wouldn't you know it, here you are, reading my book. By the way, I'm available to travel on your dime and write about fly fishing in Russia, surfing in Tahiti, or spelunking in New Zealand. Hit me up.

Shep's Official Rules of Travel:

1. **Have an overprotective parent:** When I started traveling, my dad purchased Global Rescue for me, which allows for me to be medevaced out of any country in the event of an accident (thanks for the confidence, Dad). And he didn't stop there. He went to the State Department website and printed out a list of every possible danger, depending on the country I was visiting. I still get emails from Global Rescue wondering if I have a broken leg or if I'm stuck on a glacier somewhere. Their whole business depends on international catastrophes, and their ethos is right in line with my dad's Chicken Little "the sky is falling" mentality. So, thank you, Dad, but I'm not sorry I haven't put this gift to good use.

2. **Just say no to the fanny pack:** This might not surprise you, but in addition to Global Rescue my dad was a major fan of the fanny pack and he encouraged me to wear one to keep money and valuables safe. He soon realized that for fashion's sake, I would never wear one. So instead he got me a money belt. In his mind there were thieves roaming everywhere, just waiting to snatch my cash. I took the money belt on my initial Ugly American trip to Europe, but never wore it. The moral of the story is—do not wear

something that makes you feel like a moron. You're just as likely to get pickpocketed in Atlanta or New York as you are in Rome. Just don't be a rube and leave your wallet hanging out or your phone sitting on a table unattended. Stay alert, even after multiple Jägerbombs.

3. **Embrace your true self:** You can be anyone you want if traveling alone. This is kind of funny to me, because I'm incapable of behaving like anyone other than my crazy self. But it is true, you're going somewhere with an absolute clean slate. What I like to do is tiptoe at first and analyze the landscape . . . then jump into the deep end.

4. **Choose your friends wisely:** Don't put your eggs in any one basket in the beginning, friend-wise. Trust me. There's a reason that certain people are eager to befriend you in a new place, and it's usually because nobody likes them and they're desperate, or they're a criminal. Be a passive observer as much as possible until you detect "your people." It sucks having to jettison someone down the road, plus it's bad karma.

5. **Never be the guy holding the weed (or anything else):** I mean, chip in financially (you don't want to be *that* guy!) and smoke away, but in an instant your life and fortunes can change if your pockets are full of illegal substances. Never forget that.

6. **Be open:** If someone has an off-the-wall idea—go for it. A small-town rodeo, a horse race, scooter rentals, naked

yoga, anything. It's what travel is all about. Don't just follow the guided tour leader, do something that sounds a little stupid or risky, because it usually turns out to be hilarious and memorable rather than stupid and risky.

7. **Meet the locals:** Meet as many locals as you can, as organically as possible. Simple advice here. Hell, if you came to Charleston and just went to the places that were advertised as cool, you'd miss out on so much! Good advice from a cool local can change your whole trip and experience.

Best

DAYS EVER

Since my whole life philosophy is about enjoying life and having fun, keeping track of epic days is a pastime of mine. I have a few "best days" of my life that I carry around with me, days when I had a smile on my face the whole time, and everything seemed new and exciting. In keeping with my love of travel, most of these happened in a foreign country.

Rome circa 2000: There were about six of us and we woke up around noon after a fun night out. We were looking for things to do in this great, historic city. We decided to rent a scooter and explore, and when we arrived at the rental shop, this amazing owner insisted on giving us an all-day guided tour of Rome on our scooters. He spoke reasonably good English and couldn't have been nicer or more knowledgeable. We all were totally sober and didn't stop laughing and learning all day. He took us up into the hills around Rome overlooking the city, and we were zooming around each other and looking around in awe. Just a great day.

Costa Rica circa 2012: One morning I went surfing with my new friends and all the best waves just came right to me, and I screamed down the line turning and laughing and eventually flying off the lip and doing a backflip into the water and grabbing my board and furiously paddling back out to get another. I probably got seven or eight great rides. My friends saw it all and were cheering me on, and also giving me shit for getting all the good waves. It was amazing. We paddled in after a couple of hours and went and ate breakfast at the surf camp, a delicious eggs Benedict with avocado. I tell you this, no drug or drink or anything in the world can make you feel as high as a good day surfing. You are walking on air. Then later that day, still on a high, I went into town with my buddy Jerry and sat in front of the convenience store on a dusty road and drank about seven Cuba libres and shot the shit with everyone who walked by.

Hong Kong: Remember Amber from Texas? The one who fed squid to the sharks in the Hong Kong club? We spent a day having brunch, drinking two bottles of red, flirting, and vibing all day. That was a good one.

Pebble Beach Golf Links, May 2019: I got invited by the USGA to come do a media day and play eighteen holes at Pebble Beach. I sheepishly (or brazenly) asked if I could bring a couple of friends for the round, and they kindly granted my request. My friend Carl from the Bravo show *Summer House* came out, plus Austen from *Southern Charm*. We had a strong group of miscreants. To top it off, we were paired with this lovely Instagram golf influencer Hayden, and she rode in my cart. It was a bluebird-perfect day on the most beautiful course in the world.

We had so much fun rapping with friends and staring at these dramatic cliffside views of the Pacific, not to mention flirting with the stunner in my cart. Just a great time. We ended the round and got some wonderful Napa red wine and sat by a fire and had a feast, and laughed all evening. Hard to beat that. I know what you're wondering, and for the record, she retired to her room alone, much to my chagrin.

Mexico City, 2019: I met a lovely and sophisticated Mexican lass via some friends and she offered to take me around the city the next day. We went to this Mayan museum, which was fascinating and hilarious, mainly because I kept on making little comments that had my companion half disapproving/half laughing—my favorite reaction. Then she took me to this cool out-of-the-way neighborhood for the best tacos in the city. We started to drink a little wine while bar-hopping, met up with some of her friends, and just had a great day. We topped it off with a sake and sushi dinner in Mexico City, which was as good as any Nobu. Then we kissed in front of her apartment building. She was well-behaved, unfortunately. But it was quite a day. Full disclosure, I did go out with my friends afterward and took a girl home, but that wasn't necessarily the memorable part.

August 2020: Not the best summer in general, because of the whole global pandemic thing, but one weekend I had two of my oldest and best friends up to my parents' mountain house for golf and relaxation. My parents are close with these friends as well—I guess they appreciate the fact that we were able to survive all our shenanigans over the years. I also had Craig (the human) and the girl he was seeing, and as the cherry on top, my girlfriend Taylor's weekend opened up and she hopped in the car with Craig and company. We had a full house. Not everyone had met before, but I love connecting friends and it typically works out great. The guys all woke up early to play golf and had lots of fun, everyone played decently, and Craig got to know my old school friends. The conversation was wonderful and funny. We then grabbed the girls, who had been drinking coffee and chatting with my parents on the back porch, and we all went to a great country store called Christa's, where I made them all order the same sandwich (pulled chicken on a yeast bun with bacon, pepper jack cheese, onions, coleslaw, and a heaping portion of BBQ sauce) because I think it's the best in the state. Afterward we went to a rock slide that I had gone to my whole childhood. Now, some would view this as a down moment, but I don't: I got us lost on the trail to the slide. Very lost. We almost had a casualty when one of the girls slipped, and Craig and I were predictably screaming at each other. But what worthwhile journey to paradise isn't chock-full of obstacles and pitfalls? Hasn't everyone read Homer's *Odyssey*? So we finally arrived at the slide and had nonstop laughs and group sliding for hours. We managed to survive the hike back to the car, stop at a winery, and then everyone congregated back home to cook a tenderloin and laugh all night about our day and our funny old stories. Perfect end to a perfect day.

· CHAPTER 8 ·

WHAT WOULD LIL CRAIG DO?
(WWLCD)

Lest you think I'm a vagabond heathen who can't handle an ounce of responsibility, on November 6, 2018, I became a changed man. Someone came into my life and touched my heart, and I will never be the same again.

That someone is my French bulldog, Lil Craig.

Before that fateful day, I'd talked about getting a dog, but in keeping with my natural laziness and desire to keep things status quo, I was dragging my feet. I did poke around a little bit, and before I knew it I got an email notifying me that there was a little spud an hour and a half away in Orangeburg, South Carolina, waiting to be adopted by someone who could give him a life of decadence and luxury and human food.

I called my friend (and ex–*Southern Charm* castmate) Cameran, and off we went. I'll never forget that drive to meet my future pup. I was full of nervous energy, and Cam and I had a great talk about life and responsibility. We laughed a ton. Whenever I think about it, I smile nostalgically. It didn't hurt that we got to meet Lil Craig's mom and dad and little sister pup. It was just one of those A-plus days that you don't forget. The only reason it's not on my "Best Days" list is that it was also terrifying! I was becoming responsible for another life.

I wanted a French bulldog because my friends Trey and Teeny have one, and when they'd throw cocktail parties this little monster would waddle around wanting to play with everyone, just stealing all of our hearts. Who doesn't love a little waddling ball of joy? So that's where the idea started. Before Cam and I drove out, I'd seen a few videos of my future puppy, sent by the owners. They called him Remy, short for Remington, because they said he acted like he'd been shot out of a rifle. I liked the wordplay, but I also knew it would provide maximum hilarity if I named him after my two-legged friend Craig. I also knew it would mess with fans of *Southern Charm* who see Craig and me squabbling on the show all the time, and who might not realize that our fights are buoyed by years of friendship.

On that day in November 2018, I walked in with Cameran, and there was a tiny little brown puppy, which was the sister. Then there was the mom, who was really sweet, especially after giving birth to seven puppies eight weeks prior! I'm sure she was exhausted! Then the owners asked if I wanted to meet the dad, so, being the Southern gentleman that I am, I said of course. The dad was like a bowling ball. He ran into the room and knocked everything over within seconds. I thought about taking them all, but I stuck to my guns, and when Lil Craig waddled out to meet me, I knew he was my guy. Cameran immediately insisted that I put him under my shirt and do skin-to-skin contact, like you do with human babies—so I did! His little heart was beating so fast, and so was mine. It was a big moment for us both!

So, like most pup owners, I love my dog. But if you really want to have your noodle baked, consider the fact that I started an Instagram page for Lil Craig for fun (find him @goodboycraig). Less than a year after I started it, he had gained over 90,000 followers! What a world. As I write this, I'm looking around the room for Lil Craig because I feel like that little smooshed face of his (a cross between a rabbit, Winston Churchill, a monkey, and a pig) might inspire me, but alas he is currently living it up at doggy day care.

Soon after I got the little sucker, I asked my friend Jenny in Los Angeles what she does with her dog during the day, mostly because she is a writer and she works from home. She told me that she has her pup in doggy day care because you start to feel guilty if you're working and you aren't giving them attention or exercise for a few hours. So, if I have a busy day, I'll drop Lil Craig off at My Three Dogs day care. The fact that he yanks me excitedly toward their door when I drop him off but then goes ape-shit happy as if I saved his life when I pick him up is a little perplexing, but I grade it as a net positive. They did request that I get Craig neutered after a handful of visits, so he must have been peacocking around like the coolest, most handsome dude in the club. That's my boy!

Usually, though, I take Lil Craig everywhere I go, and I pretend like he's my emotional support, which in some ways he is. Most places in my hood have basically adopted him as a little mascot, and I have a network of girlfriends who wait tables and bartend who beg to take Lil Craig for a night. I guess I've made myself second fiddle in our household. Dammit if Lil Craig isn't the king of the castle nowadays! Women love him.

Honestly, I have to admit that part of the reason I got Lil Craig was Instagram. I kept seeing photos of all these people cuddled up on couches or playing with their little furry friends, and I got jealous. If I was hungover watching movies, I wanted a little spud next to me, staring at me adoringly. Instagram made it all look so idyllic and easy. How naive I was! That's like looking at a mom's picture on Instagram where her kid is holding up a sign saying they're going to first grade, and you start longing for a kid without considering what a pain in the ass it was to get that kid out of bed, clothed, and fed. It turns out dogs are a lot of work, and they require a ton of planning and attention. Still, I can't imagine not having Lil Craig in my life. He just provides so much entertainment. For a restless and hyper soul like myself, dog ownership should have been a no-brainer. The problem was that I never felt like I had my roots deep enough in any one place to take on a pet.

When I first moved to Charleston it was a magical place of wine, women, and song, but it's also a tough place to make a living. It's easy to run out of money because you're partying too much.

You have to be entrepreneurial and disciplined to survive there, and those weren't my strong suits early on. After traveling around the world, though, I realized that Charleston was always at the top of my favorite places. Plus, that area is just in my blood, and I need to live near the ocean. Once the show happened, living there became a reality (no pun intended). Once I figured out that Charleston would be my home base in perpetuity, the decision to get a dog was simple. Plus, my folks are nearby, and I have a whole village here ready to take Lil Craig if I need to leave town at a moment's notice. It's the perfect scenario for a (mostly) responsible pet owner.

To go even further back: Before I got Lil Craig, I was speaking with one of my best buds, Tony, who lives ten minutes from me. We've known each other forever, and I commented about wanting a dog, and he chimed in that he was thinking about that as well. We had a few more beers and decided we would somehow become co-parents of a dog one day. We may be the only straight men who co-parent a dog. I'm proud of that. We're breaking barriers! The decision was more palatable because Tony is always down for parental duties. He's the disciplinarian and I'm the fun/zany one. I celebrate when Lil C acts rambunctious, just like I was/am. I will also have full-on conversations with the little guy for twenty minutes, giving him unsolicited (obviously) advice and constructive criticism, but I'm also careful to bolster his confidence and mention how excited everyone has been with his progress. A typical supportive parent.

One thing that I get asked from time to time is: Did you get Lil Craig as some sort of ploy and/or plot device for *Southern Charm*?

It's a fair question, but as any of my friends on the show can tell you, I have not and will not ever do or say anything I don't mean to get in good graces or look a certain way. I'm the ultimate "what you see is what you get" person. I've done or said some dumb and insensitive things, but I like to think I own it and on the whole I'm a forthright and dependable guy. Any questions about whether I actually got a dog so I'd appear more "likable" on camera will be met with an emphatic NO. Yes, the producers spurred me into action, but I like to think we don't have to rely on gimmicks on *Southern Charm*. The show has been on so long and some crazy drama or plot twist always seems to come up organically to keep people interested and watching. I mean, Kathryn had two kids on TV! You can't script that! Well, you can, but she didn't . . . at least, I don't think so. You'll have to ask her.

On another note, I realize that devoting an entire chapter of this book to my dog and not my girlfriend might be a bad idea— and I take full ownership of it. But I think I'll be forgiven. It isn't indicative of my feelings in any way. I feel differently and strongly about both. But I mean, I met Lil Craig first, and Lil C, if you're reading this, you were the catalyst for my human relationship to even happen, you little fury Buddha.

In some part thanks to Little C, I met my girlfriend, Taylor. It was at a restaurant with Lil Craig, and she was fairly new in town, and I thought I had met everyone within a hundred miles of Charleston. I saw her and we were both with friends and we just all got together and had a few drinks and laughs (she lied and told me she was a marine biologist who specialized in shark sex, so it was destiny that we come together). The next day I left to travel throughout Mexico for three weeks, but we stayed in touch. During the coronavirus lockdown we only had two or three quarantine fights (depending on who you talk to), and one was over a heated game of Monopoly. It's been an interesting and ultimately lovely adjustment for me, and a small taste of domestic bliss during this otherwise shitty global pandemic thing. I think Lil Craig helped me, dare I say, slow down, and that got me in the right mindset for a relationship.

I hadn't been in a relationship for several years, so I had to readjust my lifestyle a little, but it's been really very nice. Once COVID-19 hit our shores and we started playing house, the experience was overall positive. One problem, and I'm not exaggerating, is that just like Lil Craig, she has superseded me in popularity. All of my friends are going over my head and around my back to make plans (then Taylor just tells me where to go and when, which is actually fine by me). She's beautiful, kind, caring, and a wizard in the kitchen. And she loves Lil Craig like no other (maybe more than me). She keeps threatening to dognap him if something were to go awry. I hope it doesn't, for many reasons, not just because I may lose my dog.

Look, I'm honoring the two most important mammals in life! They've seen me at my worst and best, and stayed with me even when I'm drooling on the couch half-asleep on a Sunday afternoon. Neither of them have run away . . . not yet, anyway.

You see, dear reader, I'm not all about selfish debauchery. Well, yes, in many ways I am. But I'm capable of more, and of embracing the burdens of being a normal responsible adult/human being. For you see, I've basically spent forty years chasing my every whim, and now I've peered into the abyss of adulthood and the white picket fence of existence—and it didn't scare me! The point is that I'm happy today, right now. I'm trying to be present (thanks, Dr. Jardin! My therapist . . .). It's working for me, and in many ways, I have Lil Craig to thank. He lives in the moment, like most animals, and we should all try to be more like our dogs. There's a line I love from the Elton John song "I Guess That's Why They Call It the Blues" that says:

Live for each second without hesitation
And never forget I'm your man . . .

When Lil C repeatedly jumps into a rushing river, which he has done often, even though he can't swim very well, I can't get mad at him. I've jumped into many a metaphorical rushing river, and I've managed to keep my head above water! This applies to (human) relationships, too. If I'm staying in (on an extremely rare night) and Taylor is out on the town, I say dance on the bar and live in the moment, just try not to embarrass me, yourself, or our relationship while you're spittin' in the devil's eye, as they say. Really the only thing she can do to embarrass me is show too much PDA (public display of affection), because I'm not a PDA guy—unless I'm watching one of my buddies with a girl, because in that case it's hilarious. In any case, projecting into the future with relationships is a fruitless task because there are just too many variables, and Lil C reminds me of that every single day, which in turn helps me in my relationship with Taylor, since it reminds me to stop worrying about what *might* happen and focus on right now. To use a corporate buzzword, it's a symbiotic relationship.

In any case, I told one of my sober friends the title of this book, and he liked it, saying that lowering the bar is the key to life. He also said that there's a saying in Alcoholics Anonymous that goes like this:

Expectations are premeditated resentments.

I love that. It means keep it simple and live in the now. I feel like that's how Lil Craig lives. So, I'm following his example and hoping that one day, I can be as evolved as him.

Top Five Lil Craig Moments:

1. Picking him up with Cameran. He was so little and scared when I put him in my car. And frankly, I was, too! I was now responsible for this life. It was a totally exhilarating and vulnerable moment for all of us.

2. The first month I had him, he violently barfed on my dad. Once I stopped laughing (sorry, Dad) I picked him up and he barfed on me! My dad and I took Lil Craig to the pet hospital at 2:00 a.m. It was kind of neat because I was

with the man who probably took me to the hospital several times as a child, so it was a generational thing of sorts, coming full circle. Poor Lil Craig got a shot of saline in his back, causing him to swell so that he looked like Quasimodo, aka the Hunchback of Notre Dame. Here's a picture that captures the moment.

3. Let me be clear: I think dudes who get dogs to get chicks are douche bags—that being said, it does work. I went to a dog-friendly music festival called "Woofstock" (ha-ha) and got three different sets of numbers to arrange a "playdate." Those were good times, before I met Taylor, and I have Lil Craig to thank.

4. Lil Craig is good for business. A company called Farmer's Dog paid me (Lil Craig's council and executor) to do a couple Instagram posts, and it was not a small sum. I know what you're thinking, but I did not spend it. I put it in his college fund, in case he decides to follow in my footsteps and attend the University of Georgia one day.

5. In the morning when I wake up (well, midmorning), he is curled up against my legs. He won't come when I want him to and he thinks everything is always a game, but he must love me, because he's always right there. When I come home, he's always at the top of the stairs, ready to give me an excited high five when I walk up! He truly is an incredible dog.

Bachelor Pad
NECESSITIES

Besides having a dog as alluring as Lil Craig shuffling around your house, I have a few staples for a comfortable, but not too fancy, home. On this topic, I kind of am an expert:

1. A sectional and comfortable couch. I sleep on my couch half the time and love posting up there for hours (and maybe even days) at a time.

2. No roommates. I haven't had a roommate since college, besides when Whitney and I shared a beach house. It's important to have a fortress of solitude.

3. A decently stocked wet bar and some mixers. Should be self-explanatory.

4. Frozen pizza in the freezer and some soup in the cupboard. I'm no chef.

5. A well-performing and comfortable toilet will save your life. Also a good shower with a little space and good flow.

6. If you live near a beach, try to build an outdoor shower. You'll thank me.

7. A decent-size flat-screen TV and a reasonably good cable package with movie channels. I know everyone is off cable, but dammit, I'm a traditionalist on this one.

8. A guest room. It's always nice to be able to host friends from time to time.

9. Keep it minimal: Don't have too many nice things or conveniences. Keep it spartan and simple. If you impress a girl too much, she may never want to leave!

10. And finally, and this can be tough—don't host parties. Attend them. Cleaning up sucks, and even the best-intentioned people treat your shit poorly.

· CHAPTER 9 ·

CANCEL ME

I want to get something off my chest that might save a select few people a lot of time and energy: I've done and said things that make me cringe and that have literally made me toss and turn with embarrassment and regret. Nothing violent at all, but words can be weapons. So can an Instagram post.

I am not asking you to pity me, just to hear me out.

As you know if you've been reading this book, I am from the South, and, some would say the Deep South. My mom's family is from Montgomery, Alabama, and my dad's is from Camden and Boykin, South Carolina. Thankfully my relatives were well educated, well traveled, and compassionate, and I never heard words of prejudice in our household. But obviously I didn't spend my life just in my own house. I went to boarding school in Virginia,

I spent lots of time hunting and fishing all over the region, and then I headed to college at the University of Georgia. You better believe I've encountered racism and bigotry since I was old enough to know what it was. I have done and said insensitive things in the past. A couple very public things (like the story I mentioned of posting an insensitive video on Instagram where I yelled "nice cans" at a homeless woman), but a whole lot more privately.

In my youth I've been around people who have uttered completely misogynistic, racist, and homophobic jokes, and I definitely have said a few myself (I am not proud of this). At the time I/we thought it was funny to put other people down. It was mostly born of insecurity and pathetic attempts at humor and trying to be accepted into some invisible club. I also went to several parties in college and in my twenties where there were people in blackface. I've never done it myself, but I shook my head and rolled my eyes. I rarely stood up to anyone who said or did something particularly cruel. Although I do remember being defensive of kids who were picked on by friends and acquaintances. In Bible school as a little tyke, I attempted to beat up a kid who was two years older than me because he picked on my best friend (one of the few physical altercations I've experienced). It turns out the kid's mom was a teacher at the Bible school. Oops. I don't regret it, though.

During my time, I'm sure I've done some picking-on myself, mostly on my little brother and his friends, and Craig (the person, never the dog). Despite that, I can assure you everyone is alive and happy with each other at the present time. In truth, though, I've actually been on the other side of bullying, and it sucked. When

I started boarding school, I was the new guy, and my roommate T. Gil was an athlete from Philly. He was a badass on the court and in the field, but he wasn't the nicest of dudes, at least initially. He and one of his buddies would pick on me pretty mercilessly, and it made me feel two feet tall. I didn't want to go back to my dorm room, which was my new home! Plus, it was my first time away from my parents. It wasn't fun, but I did learn from it. And he and I ended up becoming best buds and we still love catching up today. He just had to get to know me and stop being so much of a dick!

I've tried and am still working on erasing insulting words or phrases from my vocabulary, and I try to correct people who say things that I feel aren't okay. Again, I'm not saying I am perfect or even close to it, but I am trying to evolve, and I'll continue to do so.

For the troll army and the keyboard warriors who want to spend time digging up dirt on me in order to cancel me, everything is already out there, and I am trying to get better. You don't deserve the (probably ill-advised) free research I have provided here, but you're welcome. I honestly think we cannot progress without an honest and frank discussion about things in the past and present that make some uncomfortable. In my opinion, to move forward we have to be honest and open, and I believe "cancel culture" impedes this by making people scared to broach any discussion of prejudice. It's just too risky to be misinterpreted. This isn't what we should be doing. Open discourse and freedom of speech are at the center of our country. If you shame someone into silence, how are they going to learn? How are you?

I'm not saying I'm a saint. Far from it. But I do try to put some good into the world. I've happily donated to numerous charities. I've worked in soup kitchens in downtown Charleston delivering food. I've created friendships online with a bunch of service members and sent them lots of care packages in Afghanistan and Iraq. I've helped raise tens of thousands of dollars for a local fourteen-year-old hero of mine named Sydney Fowler who suffered paralysis and whose family needed to make their house more handicap friendly (Hi, Syd!). I've helped raise thousands of dollars for hurricane victims in the Virgin Islands and the Bahamas by selling Shep Gear hats and shirts, and I've arranged for a huge lumber company to send materials free of charge to the Bahamas to help them build again. Also, not that this is a tangible public good and obviously it's hard to quantify, but I feel like *Southern Charm* maybe gives people in hospital beds or in the middle of particularly tough and depressing times a reason to just smile or get lost in some reality TV drama for a little bit.

One of my best friends, Josh, passed away recently after a three-year bout with cancer, and he wrote me this after the season six reunion last year. I had had a rough season and was getting it from all sides on social media:

> *Hey buddy—I thought you were great last night. The Bravosphere is clearly trying to play the Hero/Villain story and create some wild character arc with you. Let your light shine throughout all this shit. You are, at your core, an extremely intelligent human being and a force for good in the world.*

I appreciated your notation of the 6 billion year old Planet we travel throughout the Universe and that none of this bull shit really "matters." Reality TV has people trapped in some kind of warped-truth, social media point-scoring syndrome.

Anyway, I'm fighting my ass off to stay alive. I don't have a great prognosis, but rooting for you on TV helps keep my mind occupied and renders the needles and chemo bags less significant. You are a generous friend to your actual "friends."

Thank you for being my friend. Call me sometime when I'm in the hospital and let's share a laugh. Cheers.

As I reread this and cry in the corner of a coffee shop where I'm writing on my computer, it is not lost on me that this wonderful and caring message from a friend was sent after a rough patch of MINE on television, while he was fighting for his life and full of tubes in a hospital bed. RIP Josh Adams. One of the greats and a legend in my eyes.

Now, maybe you're ready to send a hate tweet about me for thinking that *Southern Charm* could possibly be a force of good in the world (maybe you already sent the tweet). That's your problem. I'm not writing this to garner praise, but to show that people are fallible and imperfect (except maybe Tom Hanks, aside from that Vegemite imbroglio). Some of us are resistant to change, and these people are the most dangerous and hard to fathom. I truly believe they're not all lost causes. Most of us are hopefully willing to change, improve, and evolve as a human being and as society changes and people rightly voice their displeasure with the way things are or with certain words that hurt them. Sometimes it's things that other cultures didn't even consider, and we need to recognize that. This isn't "safe zone" talk, but just recognizing that something hurts another human being and doing your best to curtail those things is a positive change.

This is something I'm paraphrasing from Sam Harris's *Making Sense* podcast: The definition of wisdom is recognizing the turmoil within yourself and zooming out on yourself and knowing that there are contradictions, and trying to figure out those contradictions. Cancel culture is the opposite of this. It's zooming in on something and not taking things or people as a whole. For some reason I'm reminded of the great book *To Kill a Mockingbird*. The little girl Scout Finch sees a white man who is a part of a mob that's about to invade the prison and lynch a wrongly accused black man, Tom Robinson. She calls out this man's name in the mob and says that she's friends with his son in school. It stops everything and defuses the situation, all because of a certain humanity expressed by a child. I think it's beautiful (and it's also my mom's favorite book and moment). It shows just how absurd the prejudices and hatred of adults can be.

Prejudice and racism are learned behaviors, and maybe I'm foolishly optimistic, but I hope that we as a society become more accepting of each other, and that hatred dies a little more each day. I know hatred and prejudice will never disappear, unfortunately. Some humans will always need to put others down to try and lift themselves up. That's a pragmatic view of things. Certain groups of people will need to think others are inferior so they don't feel like they're on the bottom rung of the ladder (when that mindset is actually what puts them there). And not to get too global and economic, but there are astounding wealth gaps and brutal discrimination all over the world, including our beloved America.

Buffett (Warren, not Jimmy) has a quote that goes, "It takes twenty years to build a reputation and five minutes to ruin it." He was talking about the former investment firm Salomon Brothers, but still. Now more than ever, he is right, and I think this is a big problem that we face. That of the "cancel culture." In case you have been reading along and you still don't know what that phrase means, the trusty internet/Dictionary.com describes it like this:

Cancel culture refers to the popular practice of withdrawing support for (canceling) public figures and companies after they have done or said something considered objectionable or offensive. [It's] generally discussed as being performed on social media in the form of group shaming.

Now let me describe it as I see it:

It's a demonization intended to end one's career/standing and make them suffer great reputational or financial loss. And its complete mob rule, with pitchforks and burning torches (in the form of tweets and comments). Think Salem witch trials or McCarthyism. It often ignores context, nuance, spirited debate, and real discourse over inflammatory topics, and it blasts full-speed ahead before considering if the actions or words actually did real damage. It's typically a bunch of self-appointed hall monitors or online policemen, and sometimes detectives (that's when they go back in time to uncover anything one has said over the course of their lives). They are hoping and praying for any sort of gaffe committed by someone with notoriety. And then they move on to the next victim. It gives anonymous people some feeling of agency and importance that intoxicates them.

Let me be clear, though, because I've done a lot of thinking on the topic and I try to consider all angles. I also want to explore the causes, and the people who embrace canceling. But first, a caveat: Some of you might say, *But what about people like Bill Cosby and Harvey Weinstein, don't they deserve to be canceled, and worse?* Believe me, I was elated to see those two get prosecuted in an actual court *and* in the court of public opinion. Those were real, criminal cases with many victims coming out in public. To me, that's not cancel culture, that's justice. Cancel culture, to me, isn't about something criminal, it's about reputation or behavior, and it's often about the mob tearing someone down without a thought.

If Cosby is a roaring fire, the cancel culture victim is a barely glowing ember—with a handful of people blowing on it and trying to add more wood. Sometimes it works and a full fire rages unnecessarily and without validity. And then people pick it up and just read the salacious headline and not the fine print and it spreads and then someone is finished/canceled when all it really might have been was a poor choice of words or actions that they could learn and grow from, but now they are toasted and roasted and there's no going back.

Let us try to figure out how we got here, though. If you look closely it isn't too difficult. I'm sure we are all familiar with the old saying from the network and print news "If it bleeds it leads," which means, cover the violent or scary subject first, because fear gets clicks and views. That's what the viewer wants. It's the same mentality as rubbernecking when you pass by a wreck. In today's culture, there's absolutely zero shame when it comes to feeding salaciousness, outrage, gratuitous contrarianism, blood, guts, conspiracy theories, out-and-out lies—you name it. News is a business and the name of the game is to not only reach as many viewers as possible, but to piss people off and get them angry, which then makes them more engaged and keeps them watching and retweeting.

One night I was reading an article online about Ariana Grande fans trying to cancel Lizzo over some perceived slight (full disclosure, I know very little about either of these pop stars except for this). Supposedly one of Lizzo's songs made a "top 10" list, but Ariana fans said the only reason the song did so well was because Ariana Grande sang on the track. Awful insults were being lobbed by maniac Ariana fans. It was like a firestorm, and very mean-spirited. Then I looked up at the TV to see *NBC Nightly News*, and Lester Holt said something like, "Coming up: Why these 911 dispatchers who screwed up an incoming call are now getting fired!" Just more outrage and blame to keep people watching and reading the news. People love these stories, whether they're about pop stars or 911 scandals, and I guess I do, too. It's hard to look away.

And who can forget the hilarious footage on the Weather Channel, where some of the correspondents look like they're on the verge of being sucked out of a fuselage at thirty thousand feet, and then two guys walk by smoking a cigarette as if nothing is wrong. Or when there's a hurricane and they're telling everyone to stay inside OR THEY'LL DIE! But then there's the correspondent in their rain jacket, with their hair whipping in the wind as they risk their very life to tell you how everyone is going to perish. People tune in when violence, death, or desperation is on the horizon. The news (any and all kinds) feeds the people what they want. Like a tiger getting red meat. And this is all a trickle-down effect, straight from the top. We'll show you what to be outraged about! The more lurid, the better. I feel as if we are on the brink of the end of civility (and maybe civilization!) and when you take out civility and strip it away you have a potential ticking time bomb (lots of them, actually) just ready to explode.

We are aware of the combustible environment that has been created, fostered, and squeezed for maximum profit. But who are the people who are the catalysts and wannabe people of import, the bottom of the rung whistleblowers and haters? It should come as no surprise that they are from the extremes. And I'll get into that in a second because there's definitely a big political component, which I'm about to attempt to tackle (much to the horror of my publisher). But first I want to share a story I heard on the *Howard Stern Show* (my favorite) where he talks about this woman who was formerly in a hate group who turned her life around and who now does work with the less fortunate. What she said is that on a certain level, being in that group was about finding a sense of belonging. Yes, the ties that bound them were ugly and awful, but at the end of the day it was about being part of a club. Before she got involved with the group she was lonely, depressed, and unhappy, and then she joined and she was invited places, she started dating within the group, and she felt accepted. I do believe there's a correlation here with the troll/cancel culture world. If this woman had just been canceled and shamed, she probably wouldn't have been motivated to turn things around and do some good in the world. The problem with cancel culture is it never allows forgiveness, and it never gives people a chance to learn from their mistakes.

Many of the people doing the canceling are deeply unhappy and dissatisfied with life. They want to feel important, useful, and noticed, even if what they're doing is ugly, irrational, hurtful, and destructive. They feel a part of something. I love this alleged story about a professional boxer who was getting attacked on Twitter by some guy for God knows what, but the troll said some crazy things and even mentioned the boxer's son. So the boxer did a little research and found where the guy lived. He knocks on the door, ready to fuck this guy up, and the troll just breaks down and sobs as soon as he opens the door. He admits that he doesn't know why he said those things, he's just really unhappy. The boxer took pity on him and actually ended up trying to comfort him. I'm not sure if all online trolls are redeemable, but that story gives me hope, even if it is just a virtual urban legend.

So now on to the political troll/cancel culture breakdown, according to yours truly:

You have the crazy right-wingers who are just rabid. The people who Trump was talking about when he said, "I could stand in the middle of Fifth Avenue and shoot somebody and I wouldn't lose any voters." They're the people who go to his rallies and wear the "Fuck your feelings" shirts, but if you dare criticize their dear leader or just point out a shortcoming or gaffe, they get insanely aggressive, angry, and pugilistic. They call moderates and anyone on the left snowflakes, but goodness they seem to have thin skin for people claiming to be so tough. They love saying "triggered!" thereby celebrating the fact that people are upset over a particularly cruel or idiotic deed, but they'll fly off the handle if a Dem screws up or insults a GOP leader.

Then on the other side we have the progressive crowd. I know that "progressive" has a generally positive connotation, and being open to change and new norms is a good thing. But some of these people are their own worst enemy, and they might just be the biggest and craziest faction of the cancel culture. They are offended BY EVERYTHING. They'll sift through anything and find something so obscure or inconsequential, and latch on to it like a pit bull. And then they try to accumulate support and outrage via exaggeration and removal of certain facts or context. The danger of this is that it's like the boy-who-cried-wolf syndrome. There are legitimate things that are outrageous and offensive, which should be addressed and changed. But when you yell and scream about everything, you lose the weight of some important messages.

There's a loud faction of the left that is so idealistic that they won't accept the support of people in the middle because their beliefs aren't as strong on various issues. It is crazy! One thing I know about this country is that you need the people in the middle to win elections, and if you don't win elections, they'll be little to no change and progress. Politics is a give and take. You take two steps forward and one back. You decide what's most important and prioritize it, but don't shame others just because they have a different opinion. Don't get excited (or horrified)—I have no plans to run for office or become a politician. This is just a topic that I feel passionate about, as you can see.

Despite my (winking) philosophy of living up to average expectations, that's always been more about career and personal choices. The expectation for me, my siblings, and my cousins was to be good human beings and listen to and consider other people's opinions and views and backgrounds. In that regard, being as good a citizen of the world as you possibly can, while also knowing that mistakes will be made and perfection is unattainable, has been an unspoken mantra in my life. So even though I'm a proponent of lowering the bar when you can and living a gloriously average life, becoming a more enlightened and understanding and accepting human being (one who does not cancel people without really digging into the facts and who takes time to hear someone out) is one area of life where I say, strive to be better than average. At least try for average, plus one.

P.S.: After my own brush with cancellation, when I posted the "nice cans" Instagram story that ignited the masses, I wrote this in the Notes app on my phone. I'm not sharing it to garner praise, but just to give you a glimpse into what it was like:

As I drive to Charlotte to get on a plane to Alaska, I keep replaying things in my head. The last thing I want is sym-

pathy but it's been rough and today I met up with some fans while grabbing a sandwich and it was nice and gave me a rare moment of relief. They don't care, they don't follow gossip sites. They've enjoyed you on TV and you've made them smile.

I did everything wrong from the very beginning and I just re-examine it over and over again. One minute you can be weird and try to be funny a little bit walking down the streets in New York and have a little audience with you and then bam, wrong decision, situation, all of it. But damn, the rage response is so hateful, so mean . . . saying I should kill myself, and I'm scum of the earth. How does this add up . . . Sort of a two-wrongs-don't-make-a-right situation? Creating a pretty damn ironic situation, which is, I bet many of the cancel culture people think they are protecting a victim, or acting on their behalf in a good way. And in doing so they become the predator.

· CHAPTER 10 ·

HAPPY ACCIDENTS

My life has pretty much been a series of happy accidents, and *Southern Charm* is no exception. I had no idea that going to a rooftop party in Charleston one night all those years ago would lead to me meeting Whitney, and then to being on TV. Back then, nobody could have predicted the show's popularity, at least nobody on the cast. Most of us just thought we were trying something out for a laugh, and that we'd be back to regular life soon enough. But here we are.

The first *Southern Charm*–related happy accident for me was running into Thomas Ravenel at that rooftop party on New Year's Eve and then having him introduce me to Whitney Sudler-Smith. My "interview" for the job of being on *Southern Charm* was pretty much just to be myself, get drunk, and go to a strip club. I didn't need my wildly embellished résumé or even a suit and tie, so maybe it was fate. If the job fits, do it as long as you can.

From the moment I met him at that fateful party, Whitney and I connected immediately. I just think he's a completely unique and hilarious person. Sometimes I describe him as a guy who is content to be miserable. Nothing is ever up to his specifications and lofty standards, but he's so funny about it that you almost look forward to his discontent. He is also extremely generous. One of my favorite things about him, besides that fact that he's known for picking up tabs, is that he'll call you up on a Wednesday and say, "Dude, come to Ibiza, we have a villa there, and it's going to be epic." So I'll tell him that sounds great and ask when he's going, and he'll say something like "This Friday!"

I know my love for travel might make me sound adventurous, or like I'm some global jet-setter, but flying to Spain on a whim isn't how I roll. I need to think about it, and plan a little. So regrettably I had to turn Whitney down about five times in a row, since dropping $3K on a last-minute ticket stings! Eventually I did take him up on one of these offers, because I was afraid he'd stop asking. He invited me to the Berlin Film Festival with a one-week notice— and I said yes! Let's just say I didn't see a single film and barely saw much sunlight. Berlin was a really cool city, though, sort of gloomy and gothic, and I loved it.

I actually think Whitney is my dad's favorite person on the show. There is a scene in season two where Kathryn bitches Whitney out on the porch on Jekyll Island, and the next morning Whitney is quietly trying to escape, and he's peeking around corners and sneaking around. My dad couldn't stop laughing because he said it reminded him of Peter Sellers in *The Pink Panther*.

If someone wrote a fictional script depicting everything that has happened on the show, no one would believe that people like us actually existed. Take Thomas. I mean, he's outrageous, he's flawed, he's larger than life and absolutely unpredictable. He can be charming as hell one minute, then angry as hell the next. One thing he always does is apologize, though. I can't count how many mean texts I've gotten from him at midnight, but I just learned to ignore them and wait for the contrite apology the next day, which I happily accept. I have mixed emotions about his absence from the show. I won't get involved with the details because it is none of my business, but I'll just say this: He put himself in a really bad position and paid for it, and he's done that a couple times. I wish him well, though, and miss talking to him about whatever he was passionate about that day or night. I also hate seeing his lingering anger and his lashing out at Patricia, since they were once very close friends and shared a lot of laughs. I do think Thomas convinced himself that she was the architect of his demise, which is absurd, in my opinion. He torched the bridge between them and he continues to firebomb it, which saddens me.

As for Cameran, Craig and I first met her at a restaurant called 39 Rue de Jean. I had just moved to Charleston, and Cameran had just decided to do the show. I remember thinking how beautiful and funny she was, a mix of sass and grace. I immediately wondered if I had a shot. She touched my leg over five times at the bar as she was telling stories and laughing. In my experience, the leg touch is a tiny positive gesture that has been the precursor to many a home run. Unfortunately, I looked over and she was doing the same thing to Craig, so maybe this was the beginning of our rivalry! It turns out that's just the way Cam is. She's touchy-feely and Southern and sure of herself. As fate would have it, she was already dating her now husband, Jason, at the time. How could I compete with a doctor who had a classic Ferrari and who made his own beer, and who was reserved, thoughtful, and a great listener? She chose wisely. I've watched Cam become a married woman with a child and a big house. It happened before my very eyes!

Even though he'll deny it, I actually think Craig has come the furthest of all of us. His evolution can be summed up by the simple phrase "know thyself." Or better yet, "embrace your eccentricities." Or, as Shakespeare wrote and our old friend Polonius remarked, "To thine own self be true." Craig finally stopped lying to everyone all the time and came clean about what he did and didn't want to do with his life. He didn't want to be a lawyer; he wants to make pillows, which I wholeheartedly support.

In case you missed it, there was an episode where Craig mailed a blank fake application to the South Carolina Bar Association so I'd think he was on top of his shit. Which is actually hilarious looking back, but completely and utterly unnecessary. I mean, with the time and effort put into looking like he was applying for the bar exam, he probably could have legitimately done it! I once walked into his apartment and he commented he'd been up since eight thirty in the morning taking care of things. What the "things" were is anyone's guess, but one of his roommates overheard that and later came to me and said Craig didn't wake up until noon. Why would I care what time he woke up? I wake up late and I don't think I need to remind everyone how important I think sleep is. It's everything! These little stupid white lies were intended to make him appear to have his shit together. I would call him out and we'd squabble, but the thing is, those lies start piling up and then things go sideways, and then you've got to keep all of the lies straight. It becomes a house of cards.

We've all been train wrecks at one time or another on the show, but the ultimate was season two for Craig. He got fired from his job, which you saw on the show, but he also did things like leave his car at the Charleston airport for ninety days. At first he forgot it was there, so he got a ride home. Then he procrastinated, and then he didn't have the money. It became an 800-pound (or $800) gorilla situation. When we went to get his car finally, it was like 850 bucks to get out! But that wasn't all. When he parked it down-town in front of his apartment that evening, he woke up to find it with a boot on it and a ticket saying he owed five hundred bucks in late parking tickets! To top it all off, he was sucker-punched and knocked out on Halloween, and he cracked his skull on the side-walk and had to go to the hospital. That part wasn't funny, and I'm glad it wasn't worse. So it was a rough few months for my friend. I thought he got off rather easily, considering all the follies and ridiculous behavior, but whatever.

My point is, Craig has come a long way. I trust him implicitly now. He tells the truth and owns his peccadillos and strangeness. He sews! I guess you can call him a "seamsman"? And he's good at it. I like the designs, and he stays focused. It's great. He also had the boldness to move to the Bahamas because he was falling into some habits he didn't like in Charleston, and he met some cool people and got a different perspective on life. I went down to visit and loved every minute of it, except the one fight we got into where I threw a cooked steak at his face. It was probably our biggest fight, but we made up about eighteen hours later. I was pissed because I felt like he was trying to make me look bad in front of his friends. It didn't help that we had been on a boat pounding beers in the sun all day. The point is, I actually listen to Craig's advice these days. He has had some valuable and helpful insights over the years and I value that. I'm not saying he should actually practice law and leave the pillow empire, but it's way more plausible than it was four years ago.

I think the best way to describe Craig's metamorphosis is this: Austen, Craig, and I share a personal trainer named Brian, aka "Swolly Mammoth." We train together, or Austen and I train and Craig sometimes shows up. Our text chain is called Biceps 4 Bravo. Anyway, one time Craig out of the blue said he was going to join us the following day, so we got excited. The next morning we were getting ready for the 11:00 a.m. session and we got a text at 10:30 a.m. from Craig saying, "Guys, I can't make it. I have a mani-pedi appointment at eleven thirty and it was the only time she could fit me in." The point is that he's owning the weirdness and embracing it. He's painting his fingernails blue, designing pillows, and going on tour to interior design stores across the East Coast. Go, Craig, go! The truth shall set him free! I love Craig 3.0. Or is 4.0? However many there have there been, this version is my favorite.

And then there is Kathryn. Oh, Kathryn. I do love and root for her, but she does make it hard at times. I first met Kathryn when we started filming the first season. She wasn't officially a cast member, but she was being invited to many of the functions we were filming. It was very obvious to me that she wanted to be in front of that camera. And why not? She's darn good at it. She's six feet tall with wild red hair. You can't *not* notice her. I remember, once, she came out to hang at the beach with me and my fun, non-show friends, and they instantly liked her. She's funny and irreverent. The first season, she wasn't officially part of the cast, but she was Thomas's girlfriend and she quickly became part of the scenes, and then the show. I think she naturally took to it and became a major cast member. That girl is strong-willed.

Also, without revealing too much, I had a wonderful time with Kathryn during our brief affair. I remember walking to the Battery downtown and sneaking a couple glasses of wine and dangling our legs over the sea wall. I remember reading my favorite passages of books to her out loud on my couch, and I remember her writing me a four-page note and leaving it on my coffee table one morning. The note was so nice and raw and real that it still makes me feel warm and fuzzy to this day. I also remember tearing each other's clothes off . . . Oh wait, I said I won't reveal too much. She was lovely and I do believe I had a calming influence on her and maybe still do.

I always see her as the girl laughing at my dumb jokes and letting her guard down to reveal a very sweet and complex person. But boy can Kathryn be her own worst enemy as well. She's got a short fuse that causes her to fly off the handle. She lets her passion get the best of her and it turns her into someone else at times. She forgets who her friends are and turns inward, believing that everyone is out to get her and she can't trust anyone. She and Thomas were like gasoline and fire. Still, we had happy accidents occur on the show with the birth of their two children. At least, I believe it was an accident. They sure seemed to indicate that it was. I would be completely dishonest if I didn't give a huge amount of credit to the both of them for our show's success. I mean, what fan isn't going to keep watching after babies are born on TV? Plus, I always joke that Kathryn is the patron saint of scorned women. Hell hath no fury!

As for Austen, I met him through my good girlfriend Bailey. He would have these wild late nights at his place back in the day and we just hit it off. He's an affable dude chasing women and drinking beers, so we had very parallel interests. Plus, he's a Phish phanatic, and I love them, too, so how bad can a guy be if he loves great music? When friends ask me what Austen is like in "real life," I simply say he went to thirteen Phish shows in a row in NYC once, and they usually just nod, acknowledging that he's one of us. I lobbied hard to get him on the show when they were looking for new people. I thought he would counterbalance Craig's sensitive nature, and we all might have a lot of fun acting up together. Well, that's been proven to be true, but I must admit I failed to properly assess Austen. Hell, he's just as sensitive and emotional as Craig, if not more so! Sometimes we all fight, or gang up on each other, but we never carry the anger around for more than about thirty minutes. You'll usually find us all laughing shortly after a blowup.

The matriarch of the show is obviously Patricia. She's Whitney's *actual* mom, but she is my mom away from home. I love her. She's extremely generous with the parties she throws and the meals and nice bottles of wine she's shared with me. She's generous of spirit. If you called and asked her to do something or help you with anything, she is always game. My parents came to visit Charleston when the show was still new, and Patricia had us to the house for cocktails. It went well, we all chatted and laughed and talked about her Virginia roots and her life experiences. It was a great time.

Well, the next day my mom called me and said, "I'm worried for Patricia." I asked why on earth she was worried. She said, "I worry about the way she is portrayed on TV. She's just so nice and lovely and that doesn't always come across on your show."

I had to laugh. My mom was worrying for my other mom! I assured my actual mom that Patricia can handle it, and that I thought she relished her role on the show as sort of the snarky somewhat ostentatious queen bee. I'm not saying she's playing a role, but she can turn it on sometimes, and I think the viewers love it when she does. What everyone doesn't see is when Whitney's home and they invite me over and we eat fried chicken or some vegetarian chili in the TV room with our feet up laughing about some ridiculous rumor or whatever. She really is one of the guys sometimes. She doesn't even wince at our vulgarities, like my real mom would.

Like any show, we've had people come and go over the years. I hated to see good friends like Cameran leave, but things change and evolve, and so does the show. I wish her all the happiness in the world and we communicate often, and we both have expressed that we'll be friends until we are old and gray. And that makes me smile.

I miss Chelsea and Naomie too, and will always consider them friends. I thought Chelsea brought a down-home feeling and real Southernness to the table. I thought and still think she's great. Chelsea, if you're reading this, I'll meet you for a surf session in Nosara very soon!

Naomie lost her dad and she had also fallen in love, and I don't think she wanted to share all of that on TV. She chose family over filming, and how can that ever be wrong? I wish her the best and will always enjoy running into her and eating amazing meals at her family's restaurant, Nico.

And then there's me. Obviously, I'm still coming back for more. When the show first started filming, I was a total piece of clay on camera. I had no idea how it all worked. Filming a TV show was a little like learning a new language, but it's a collaboration that I came to really like. It's a good feeling when you see things fall into place and it seems like they're really working. I remember when we were filming the first season and I had some witty banter going on, and I thought what I was saying was the most clever, hilarious thing ever uttered on television. I quickly learned to check my ego, but I had and still have a hell of a lot of fun going back and forth with my friends. Maybe I was naive, but naivety and optimism can be a strength. There have been moments when I feel like something is funny and compelling, and it gives me a sense of pride. That's one of the main reasons I'm still doing the show.

There have been a number of events that have occurred on the show over the years that you just couldn't even make up. These outrageous and unpredictable things have, in my opinion, compelled viewers to stay tuned in year after year. Just as no one could have predicted the show's success, no one could have foreseen the attention and sometimes harsh criticism we would all eventually receive. None of us knew how to deal or cope with it all. After all, we weren't in L.A. or New York, poking around the entertainment industry, savvy about PR or how to play "the game." Except for Whitney, who was in that world, we all learned on the fly, with varying degrees of success. We all got our comeuppance at one point or another, sometimes twice. Sometimes fully deserved, sometimes the result of a slight misunderstanding. I genuinely think that every person who has been on our show is redeemable and essentially good. Well, maybe not Thomas's ex-girlfriend Ashley.

What I'm saying is, everything isn't always as it appears on our show, although I'll put my hand to my heart as far as the veracity of our actions are concerned. We are not actors and we are not faking it. Sometimes it's tough for us to know the full story, but it's like that in everyday life sometimes too. You hear something about a friend, a rumor starts, and before you know it a story has gotten out of hand.

So, if you watch the show, please keep this in mind before you take to Twitter and tell us you wish we'd die or whatever level of hate you are serving up: Just take a deep breath and think about the context and "zoom out" on any one of us. Might there be a reason for a disparaging comment? Is there a pattern of cruel behavior in the past? Is the person a shit talker and mudslinger by nature? By the way, this should extend to all our "real" lives as well. The benefit of the doubt is the best way to approach most situations, but I guess every story needs a villain. No one would watch a movie or

TV show if it was about a bunch of people who are polite and nice and reserved 100 percent of the time.

I think most of us see the show as being a lot of fun, as I believe most of you do. So we would like to keep making y'all laugh and/or pull your hair out, or both, for many years to come.

· CHAPTER 11 ·

LAST LAUGHS

A s I've referenced several times over the course of this book, I really enjoy writing. Wait, let me rephrase that: Once I sit my hyper ass down and remove the one million distractions from my head and get on a roll at the keyboard . . . I really enjoy writing. I used to read Bill Simmons articles religiously when I was in my twenties, and here was this guy talking sports and writing about ridiculous trips to Vegas with his buddies, and I thought, I've got some of those stories to tell. On a higher level (sorry, Bill) I love David Foster Wallace, and his work had a huge impact on me. He was a hilarious writer, and I read his essay "A Supposedly Fun Thing I'll Never Do Again" when I was on a plane, and it made me laugh so hard the guy next to me thought I was crying and hyperventilating because I was upset. Really, I was just entertained by words on a page, and that seemed like a pretty good goal. I love to entertain people, so why not do it with words as well?

Then one day as I was pursuing my average but always interesting (to me, anyway) life, I got the chance to actually write a book. I found myself in New York City, where I was asked to attend a cool party during fashion week (I know, rough stuff). During that trip I met with my publisher (hi, guys), and when I walked into the building, I was legit in awe. As a book lover, I was freaking out about the framed photos of famous books that lined the halls, and imagining the authors who had walked there before me. It was amazing. I was ushered into a conference room and met with six welcoming people, and because I was in such awe (and also still kind of buzzed from the fashion part the previous night), I just rambled on about anything and everything. A few times they cut in with an idea, and I just nodded and agreed and plowed on, trying to be funny.

I sat down to write, and when I sent the first page to my agent she immediately wrote me back and said, "You realize that you agreed to do a certain type of book in the publisher's offices, right? This isn't that book!" Oh crap. What had I, in my nervous/hungover state, agreed to do?! I think I just rambled on that day and agreed to everything without really hearing anything because I just wanted them to like me. The pressure was real!

It turns out I had committed to write a tongue-in-cheek guide to being a Southern gentleman. WHAT? NO! I had important things to say, dammit! This was a serious affront to my pseudo-intellectualism. Maybe that book would have become a mega success, but it wasn't me. I'm on a show called *Southern Charm*, but I am no expert on being a Southern gentleman, although I do know how to behave at dinner parties (sometimes) and weddings (occasionally) and important events (maybe?). The point is, that wasn't me, and I didn't want to give you guys a phony version of myself. What you've just read is pure 100 percent Shep Rose, unfiltered and (semi) uncensored.

I actually started writing this book during the initial coronavirus quarantine in South Carolina. If you harbor a desire to write and you're not able to do it while stuck in your home for months, you probably should aim for another passion. I genuinely loved the experience, which might cause some writers to hate-tweet me since for many writers I know the process can be torturous. I often laughed out loud while writing and remembering certain stories, and I certainly loved polling my family and friends for any minor insanity that I may have missed. Looking over old emails and report cards and postcards that my mom had saved over the years gave me endless joy. But more than that, writing this really gave me a great sense of purpose, accomplishment, and responsibility. I know I have a reputation of being a dilettante, and I could go into detail about a lot of the things that I work on and am enthusiastic about when we aren't filming—but I won't do that to you now. You're almost at the finish line! Plus, defending yourself to trolls is like pissing in the wind. So just know that this has given me a sense of purpose and focus, which, for a forty-something man who could add "gallivanting" and "revelry" sections to my résumé, is a major accomplishment.

Often over the past year or so I've spoken to my therapist and told her what I'm up to professionally and what I'm excited about. I can be my harshest critic, because let's face it, as much as we say we don't listen to the haters, of course we all do. But my therapist was quick to tell me, "Listen, you're writing a book, you're about to film another season of your show, you're excited about a scripted show you've created and are working on with writers in L.A., you're designing and selling shirts and hats for Shep Gear. What more do you want?" Her tough love helped, especially when I thought about the book. I have a tangible piece of evidence of my hard work and passion here. I can feel it and touch it and hold it, and sleep with it under my pillow, and send it to friends, and use it for kindling (wait, strike the last one). In short, this feels good and that's one of my most important life philosophies: "If it feels good, do it." Think of me as the Socrates of leisure.

So maybe this book will fulfill or exceed my own average expectations and (gasp!) raise the bar. I really just hope I can come away from it feeling like I've made my friends and family laugh a little and swell with pride. Never mind that my nieces and nephews won't be able to read it until their late teens. Or maybe their early twenties? I don't want to send them on the same dangerous and idiotic expeditions I went on armed only with foolhardy and irresponsible philosophies. Although it worked out okay for me.

I originally wanted to call this book *You Can't Lasso a Zebra*, because, since I come from this pretty traditional Southern background, there's that old assumption that you get married, join the country club, have kids, get involved with the PTA, and then you die! And I just never even came close to that . . . yet. It turns out that apparently zebras can't be domesticated. The zebra can't be lassoed because it has been conditioned to basically have 360-degree vision so as not to get eaten by predators. I'm not saying I have 360-degree vision, but I do have 20/20 vision. Plus, I just love roaming the plains unfettered and carefree! With full knowledge that lions lurk behind every patch of grass.

So, thanks for taking a look under the hood of the car that is me. I sure hope you were as entertained reading this as I was writing it. If you like it, lend it to a friend (or tell them to get their own copy!). If you do lend it out, look your friend dead in the eye and make them promise to return it so you can read it again and again. I'm definitely not saying this book should be a guideline for any of you, but maybe a devilish smile and a dollop of adventurousness with a side order of insanity can be added to your dinner plate. Because at the end of the day, or the night, or at dawn when you're stumbling home, life is really all about having some fun, making some memories, and, most important of all, being in on the joke.

SUGGESTED READING LIST

Just when you thought you were finished with me, here I am again!

I'm sharing these because I can. And because I love books. And because I love telling other people about great books to read. So, I'll start with rock biographies, because as you will see, I'm a sucker for them:

I'll Sleep When I'm Dead by Warren Zevon: A very flawed but very talented guy, sad in the end.

Life by Keith Richards: He's a personal hero.

Scar Tissue by Anthony Kiedis: A raw and crazy book. I think in trying to rationalize his awful behavior after the fact he sounded almost worse, but still a good read.

Slash by Slash: In contrast to Kiedis, he's just as insane but just sort of owns it and shrugs. Love Slash.

The Heroin Diaries by Nikki Sixx: I had just come off a NYC bender weekend and bought this in the airport. It was exactly what I needed—at least I wasn't as fucked up as this guy! I'll throw in the book *The Dirt* about the whole band Mötley Crüe, but Sixx's book was way more personal.

Crosby, Stills, Nash and Young by David Browne: I loved reading this. This band was one of the biggest in the world for a few years, and they all had huge egos and were extremely dysfunctional. A page turner.

I Must Say: My Life as a Humble Comedy Legend by Martin Short: His biography was so damn good. I learned a ton and laughed a lot and cried like a baby at the part when his longtime wife succumbed to cancer. I actually ran into him in L.A. a few months after reading the book and told him how much I loved it. He was super nice and asked me about myself. I have no idea what I said. He's a hero.

Live from New York: The Complete, Uncensored History of Saturday Night Live *as Told by Its Stars, Writers, and Guests*: I blew through this book. It's amazing to hear all the people who have come through those doors tell their versions of events.

Star: How Warren Beatty Seduced America by Peter Biskind: This guy bedded every starlet for thirty years in Hollywood and he must have been good at it, because there was a new one waiting in the next room at all times. A legend.

No One Here Gets Out Alive by Jerry Hopkins and Danny Sugerman: This one is about the Doors and I read it in high school when I had a little obsession with Morrison. I loved how crazy he was one second and thoughtful the next. People hate on the Doors sometimes, but Jim was a total American original.

Look Alive Out There by Sloane Crosley: My literary agent gave this book to me as inspiration, and I just fell in love with Sloane Crosley's writing style and sense of humor. So, in a way, she deserves a shout in *Average Expectations*.

Monster: Living Off the Big Screen by John Gregory Dunne: It's an autobiography about the author and screenwriter trying to get his movie made and how much he gets trampled. It's both heart-breaking and hilarious.

Steve Jobs by Walter Isaacson: I read this twice. A fascinating and complex guy. Not all that nice at times, but a genius. Loved the part where he's the CEO of both Apple and Pixar, negotiating billion-dollar deals on two fronts and absolutely kicking everyone's ass. Another American original.

Barbarians at the Gate/When Genius Failed/Liar's Poker: Three different books about insanely overconfident criminal Wall Street guys. Informative and eye-opening, whether you care about Wall Street or not.

The Boys in the Boat: The True Story of an American Team's Epic Journey to Win Gold at the 1936 Olympics by Daniel James Brown: My mom gave this to me, and I wasn't sure I'd like it, but she was right. Again. It's about competitive rowing in the early twentieth century, focusing on a particular guy and team. A wonderful story and I couldn't believe how huge rowing used to be as a national sport.

Not a Good Day to Die: The Untold Story of Operation Anaconda by Sean Naylor: About an early mission in Afghanistan. They were poised for victory, until the higher-ups in Washington got involved and hundreds died because of people thousands of miles away and their thirst for glory.

Open by Andre Agassi: I was a big Agassi fan growing up, and I still love tennis. Another really complex guy. He had some super low moments but he persevered and went out a winner.

Boys Will Be Boys/The Bad Guys Won! by Jeff Pearlman: Two books, one about the 1990s Dallas Cowboys and the other about the 1986 Mets. What a bunch of insane sports stories.

Kitchen Confidential by Anthony Bourdain and *Setting the Table* by Danny Meyer: If you're interested in the restaurant business or if you wonder what happens behind the scenes as you sit at your table, read these.

Jackpot by Jason Ryan: This takes place in South Carolina, and it's about some local guys smuggling pot from Jamaica, and instead of going to Miami like everyone else, they ran their business in the tidal creeks they all knew from childhood. One of the biggest drug investigations in history.

As you can see, I love nonfiction, but here are a few fiction picks . . .

Lonesome Dove by Larry McMurtry: My mom sat me down and promised me I'd love this book, even though it's about nine hundred pages long. Boy was she right. So many rich and unique characters that you literally fall in love with from page one.

The Prince of Tides by Pat Conroy: A simply wonderful book and I think his best. Makes you laugh, cry, and ball up your fist in absolute anger. The brother is one of my favorite characters in fiction.

To Kill a Mockingbird by Harper Lee: My absolute favorite hero of fiction is Atticus Finch, and I know I'm not alone in that. I wish all Southerners and perhaps humans in general would be mandated to read this year after year.

Snow Falling on Cedars by David Guterson: Just a beautiful love story.

City of Thieves by David Benioff: Benioff is also cocreator and writer of *Game of Thrones*. This book is so lovely and inspiring. It's set behind German lines during WWII.

Every single book (early ones especially) by John Irving: He's my mom's favorite writer and she introduced me to his weird/quirky and beautiful worlds and characters that he created.

A few of my all-time favorites:

A Prayer for Owen Meany

The World According to Garp

A Son of the Circus (very underrated and fascinating book)

The Water-Method Man

Water for Elephants by Sara Gruen: Such a sweet and great story, made into a not-so-great film.

Shogun by James Clavell: This book kicks ass. It's a long read about a Viking dude who is stranded in old-world Japan. He's in a constant chess match with them while he learns their language and customs. Both sides are using each other. Lots of intrigue.

The Power of One by Bryce Courtenay: A cool story about a young boy becoming a boxer in South Africa. Uplifting and sometimes sad.

ACKNOWLEDGMENTS

Thanks to Dina Gachman, to whom I gave tacit permission to yell at me if I wasn't writing enough and who helped tremendously with this book. She asked all the right questions and pushed me perfectly, and we didn't even have to yell all that much. We actually laughed a lot, and then yelled. Big thanks also to my agents at WME, Danielle and Eve. They listened to my pontifications over lunch in NYC and came to the conclusion that I should put pen to paper. Much love, y'all!

Thank you to the Quarantine of 2020 for keeping my ass at home and giving me lots of guilt if I spent a day sitting on my couch drinking wine and not writing. If you can't write a book during lockdown, when can you? Thanks to the quarantine crew for keeping me sane . . . and healthy. Taylor and Tony, what fun we had. It will never be forgotten—unless I forget due to dementia. Thanks to Natasha Simons and Simon & Schuster for thinking I had a book in me and listening to my ramblings and ideas in a noisy bar in NYC in November 2019 (crazy to think those places ever existed). Thank you to Maggie Loughran, who worked so hard on this book, as well as Jen Bergstrom, Aimee Bell, Abby Zidle, and Jennifer Robinson.

ACKNOWLEDGMENTS

Thanks of course to all my Hilton Head people! My family, especially my mom, who is the keeper of the crypt of my insane stories. Can't tell you how many times I called her for reference or clarification. Mom, I put you through hell growing up, and now look! You can read about it and relive it! Dad, Wooze, and Katie, love y'all, and thanks for making sure I stayed alive. I'm sorry for trying to kill you in the Bahamas, Whitaker.

Also thank you to all my teachers for your patience and encouragement. I was an irascible little punk, but I had potential? Maybe. To all the school administrators, I don't thank you for anything. You were in the ivory tower and we were in the trenches. Sorry, my anti-authoritarianism is acting up again.

A big thank-you to Bravo and Haymaker and Whitney Sudler-Smith. You wouldn't be reading this if they hadn't plucked me out of Charleston and put me on TV (unless you were into really obscure memoirs). Their foresight and belief that the cast of characters on *Southern Charm* might be interesting to some people is why life is so lucky and good for me now. Also to all my fellow cast members . . . what a ride. And finally to Close Buddies I, which is my text chain with some of my oldest friends. It's a constant source of comedic entertainment and always helps me raise the idiot bar just a little higher (or lower).